THE
Sherlock Holmes
MISCELLANY

THE
Sherlock Holmes
MISCELLANY

ROGER JOHNSON
& JEAN UPTON

First published 2012

The History Press
The Mill, Brimscombe Port
Stroud, Gloucestershire, GL5 2QG
www.thehistorypress.co.uk

British Library Cataloguing in Publication Data.
A catalogue record for this book is available from the British Library.

ISBN 978 0 7524 7152 5

Typesetting and origination by The History Press
Printed in Great Britain

· CONTENTS ·

· ACKNOWLEDGEMENTS ·

WE'D LIKE TO THANK the following people who provided special assistance toward the completion of this book:

Scott Bond; Gyles Brandreth; Sue Collier and her staff at The Sherlock Holmes pub; Catherine Cooke; Michael Cox; Jeff Decker; Evelyn Herzog; Jon Lellenberg; Roger Llewellyn; Harold & Teddie Niver; Steven Rothman; Bill Vande Water; Sue Vertue, Steven Moffatt, Mark Gatiss and the *Sherlock* cast and crew; Michael Whelan and Mary Ann Bradley.

And the many friends and colleagues around the world who help to keep the memory green.

BY GYLES BRANDRETH

NO TRUE HOLMESIAN WILL want to be without this wonderful book – and I am a true Holmesian. I really am.

I am a Londoner. I was brought up in Baker Street. My parents lived in a block of flats called Chiltern Court, immediately above Baker Street tube station. It is a block with an interesting literary heritage. H.G. Wells lived at Chiltern Court. Arnold Bennett died there. From my parents' sitting-room window you looked over Baker Street itself onto what was the Abbey National Building Society headquarters, regarded by many as the location of 221B Baker Street. So, when I was a boy, Sherlock Holmes was not simply my hero: I felt he was my neighbour.

And when I left London and was sent away to boarding school, I took Holmes with me – and decided to bring him to life. At school, in my early teens, I read (and re-read) the complete Holmes canon, as well as William S. Baring-Gould's 1962 'biography' of my hero, and decided that I would write my own Sherlock Holmes drama. I wrote a play (my first play!) and called it *A Study in Sherlock*. I cast a 12-year-old friend of mine in the title role. His name was Simon Cadell and he went on to become a professional actor of distinction. You may remember him from *Hamlet* – or *Hi-De-Hi*. As Holmes, Simon, aged 12, was definitive – rivalled only (in my mind) by Jeremy Brett a few years later.

After school and university, I maintained my enthusiasm for Holmes, reading and re-reading the stories, both for pleasure and, in moments of crisis, for comfort. (Holmes, Watson and their world give us what a great poet once described as 'the security of known relationships'.) When I was a member of parliament, my happiest hours were spent curled up in a red leather armchair in the library of the House of Commons, taking refuge from the hurly-burly (or tedium) of the chamber in the company of the world's foremost consulting detective.

It was in the Library of the House of Commons that I came across the autobiography of Sir Arthur Conan Doyle. It was reading this biography (first published in 1926) that I discovered that Conan Doyle – creator of my fictional hero, Sherlock Holmes – had known (and admired) my other life-long hero, Oscar Wilde. The pair met in 1889, in London, at the newly built Langham Hotel, in Portland Place. They were brought together by an American publisher, J.M. Stoddart. Evidently, Wilde, then 35, was on song that night and Conan Doyle, 30, was impressed – and charmed. 'It was a golden evening for me,' he wrote. The upshot of it was threefold: Stoddart got to publish Arthur Conan Doyle's second Sherlock Holmes story, *The Sign of the Four*, and Oscar Wilde's novel, *The Picture of Dorian Gray*, and, more than a century later, I began writing a series of Victorian murder mysteries featuring Oscar Wilde as my detective (more Mycroft than Sherlock Holmes, of course) with Dr Arthur Conan Doyle as his Dr Watson.

And this fascination of mine with the friendship between Wilde and Conan Doyle led directly to my friendship with Roger Johnson and Jean Upton, whose remarkable *Sherlock Holmes Miscellany* you now hold in your hand – or have before your eyes, should you be reading this on a tablet. It is a truly wonderful book – entertaining, engaging, surprising – and it is the work of two wonderful people who know the world of Holmes better than anyone else I know. I thought that the meeting between Wilde and Conan Doyle, these two great literary myth-makers, merited a commemorative plaque on the exterior of the Langham Hotel – and Johnson and Upton, alongside fellow members of the Sherlock Holmes Society of London and the Oscar Wilde Society, made it happen. (When you are next in Portland Place, please take a look at the plaque. We are proud of our endeavour.)

Jean Upton was born and brought up in Wyncote, Pennsylvania, in a house formerly occupied by Christopher Morley, who, in 1934, founded the Baker Street Irregulars. At the age of 6 Jean read her first Sherlock Holmes story, 'The Engineer's Thumb'. In the 1980s she joined the Sherlock Holmes Society of London and made annual visits to Britain for the Society's weekend excursions. In 1992 she married Roger Johnson. (Rumour has it, Roger proposed at the Reichenbach Falls…) A very special guest at their wedding was Sir Arthur's daughter, Dame Jean Conan Doyle.

Roger Johnson was born and still lives in Chelmsford. He worked for nearly forty years as a librarian with Essex County Council Libraries and has been a member of the Sherlock Holmes Society of London since 1968. In 1982 he started the Society's newsletter, *The District Messenger*, which he still writes and distributes. Since 2007 he has also edited *The Sherlock Holmes Journal*. Thanks to the newsletter, he is in touch with Sherlock Holmes groups throughout the world, and holds honorary membership in societies in Australia, Canada, France, the USA and the UK.

Both Roger and Jean are members of the senior American society, the Baker Street Irregulars, and of the Adventuresses of Sherlock Holmes... If that piques your curiosity, all is explained in the chapter entitled 'You have been at your club all day' – but do not rush to it right away. Read this book from start to finish and revel in every page. It is the ultimate *vade mecum* for Holmesians everywhere. It is the one book that has been missing from the shelf of the true Sherlockian. It has got all the stuff in it that you would expect – and so much you wouldn't. It is a labour of love and a model of scholarship. Behold the fruit of pensive nights and laborious days, dear reader – and enjoy.

Gyles Brandreth,
2012

· INTRODUCTION ·

'A FRIEND OF MR SHERLOCK IS ALWAYS WELCOME'

WHAT IS IT THAT we love about Sherlock Holmes? In 1946, Edgar W. Smith, editor of *The Baker Street Journal*, attempted to explain:

> We love the times in which he lived, of course: the half-remembered, half-forgotten times of snug Victorian illusion, of gaslit comfort and contentment, of perfect dignity and grace...

> But there is more than time and space and the yearning for things gone by to account for what we feel toward Sherlock Holmes. Not only there and then, but here and now, he stands before us as a symbol – a symbol, if you please, of all that we are not, but ever would be. His figure is sufficiently remote to make our secret aspirations for transference seem unshameful, yet close enough to give

them plausibility. We see him as the fine expression of our urge to trample evil and to set aright the wrongs with which the world is plagued. He is Galahad and Socrates, bringing high adventure to our dull existences and calm, judicial logic to our biased minds. He is the success of all our failures; the bold escape from our imprisonment.

Or, if this be too complex a psychological basis to account for our devotion, let it be said, more simply, that he is the personification of something in us that we have lost, or never had. For it is not Sherlock Holmes who sits in Baker Street, comfortable, competent and self-assured: it is we ourselves who are there, full of a tremendous capacity for wisdom, complacent in the presence of our humble Watson, conscious of a warm well-being and a timeless imperishable content. The easy chair in the room is drawn up to the hearthstone of our very hearts ... And the time and place and all the great events are near and dear to us not because our memories call them forth in pure nostalgia, but because they are a part of us today.

That is the Sherlock Holmes we love – the Holmes implicit and eternal in ourselves.

It is difficult to improve upon those sentiments. We have been devoted to Sherlock Holmes from a very early age and with the recent phenomenal resurgence of interest in the 'Great Detective', we are coming into contact with many people who are only just learning about this eccentric but charming little world of ours. Some novices are interested only in films and television, others are eagerly devouring the original stories, and, gratifyingly, there are also those who wish to dip their toes in the vast ocean of canonical scholarship.

The Sherlockian world is large, with room for everyone. Back in 1971, Dr Julian Wolff – Smith's successor at *The Baker Street Journal* – made a telling comment: 'It is well known that the purpose (and delight) of the Baker Street Irregulars is to pursue the study of that great body of Sherlockian literature. Now I hope I shall not be impeached for heresy when I say that an equally great and delightful purpose is the forging of true friendships.' It is the sharing of this interest with others that makes it such fun and also keeps Sherlock Holmes alive for yet another generation.

For more than a century books have been written on the subject of Holmes and his world; it would be impossible to compress all of that information into a single, small volume such as this. It would also be idiotic to try. When describing Professor Moriarty, Holmes remarks: 'He sits motionless, like a spider in the centre of its web, but that web has a thousand radiations...' This book is intended to be like that spider, but in a good way. We've tried to provide some basic information on a number of topics with links to where you can find out more; it's then up to you to follow any of those 'thousand radiations'.

As we said, the Sherlockian world is a friendly one, so we've included quite a lot of information on its population.

If you have a specific query or are having difficulty trying to track down a particular book or reference, help is always only an email or a phone call away.

Join the Grand Game!

1

'MAY I INTRODUCE YOU TO MR SHERLOCK HOLMES?'

HOW EXACTLY DOES ONE first become introduced to Sherlock Holmes? Even if you have not yet discovered the original stories, you'll know that Holmes is omnipresent in everyday life. His name has become a byword, whether used sarcastically or admiringly, for someone who investigates matters or solves troublesome problems. His iconic image appears in cartoons, greetings cards and advertisements. His exploits are dramatised for the stage, radio, audio recordings, television and cinema screen. With the advent of the internet there are countless websites, blogs, discussion groups and tweets. Quotations from the stories have been gradually absorbed into our conversations (how often have you heard someone refer to 'the dog in the night-time'?). With the plethora of media now available, it is very nearly impossible to escape the influence of Sherlock Holmes.

But what about that initial, early awareness of the Great Detective? American children born in the 1940s or '50s would most likely have first encountered Sherlock Holmes in the Basil Rathbone and Nigel Bruce films that were enjoying a renaissance on our tiny black-and-white television screens. He also featured in the cartoons shown on children's television programmes, either as an idealised character, or with a familiar cartoon personality, togged up with a pipe, magnifying lens and deerstalker.

British children of the same generation were less aware of the films of Rathbone and Bruce until much later in life. For them, the radio series starring Carleton Hobbs and Norman Shelley paved the way to dreams (or nightmares) of adventure, soon followed by the 1960s television productions with Douglas Wilmer or Peter Cushing as Holmes and Nigel Stock as Dr Watson. Some young Britons were even lucky enough to find old forgotten copies of *The Strand Magazine* tucked away in an aged relative's attic.

Regardless of where we grew up, most of us can recall reading our first Conan Doyle-penned stories by the age of around 10 or 11. What a treat they were! Poisonous snakes, ancient rituals, daring burglaries, mysterious noises from behind the door in the tower… What more could one ask for? Well, more of the same – and what a joy it was to discover at the library or local bookshop that there *were* more. We found that the short stories were divided into delicious chunks of books: *The Adventures of Sherlock Holmes*, *The Memoirs of Sherlock Holmes*, *The Return of Sherlock Holmes*, *His Last Bow*, and *The Case Book of Sherlock Holmes*. Once these morsels were devoured, we feasted on the novellas, or long stories: *A Study in Scarlet*, *The Sign of Four*, *The Valley of Fear* and *The Hound of the Baskervilles*.

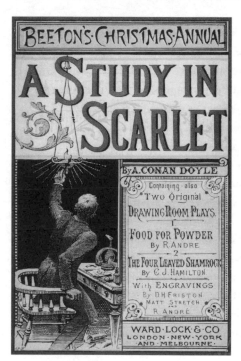

Beeton's Christmas Annual for 1887. The main feature is *A Study in Scarlet* – the first story of Sherlock Holmes. *Collection of Roger Johnson and Jean Upton*

For some brave young souls *The Hound* was the first story they read, much to the consternation of countless parents who had to deal with the results of the inevitable nightmares. Another trauma for young minds was the death of Sherlock Holmes, as recounted in 'The Final Problem'. Many adult Sherlockians of our acquaintance admit that they could never bring themselves to re-read the story, so deep-seated and memorable was the distress caused by this incident. Not even the rapture of discovering that Holmes had not perished could erase this aversion.

If you are one of those rare beasts, an adult who has not yet read the original stories, then hesitate no longer. Curl up in an armchair by the fire while twilight creeps in, prop yourself up in bed with a restorative cup of tea, laze in a shady garden or on a sun-drenched beach; regardless of where you are, Holmes is the ideal companion.

'THE BEST AND THE WISEST MAN WHOM I HAVE EVER KNOWN'

Young Stamford looked rather strangely at me over his wine-glass. 'You don't know Sherlock Holmes yet,' he said; 'perhaps you would not care for him as a constant companion.'

A Study in Scarlet

What is so special about Conan Doyle's creation, and how has he so adeptly endured the test of time? Holmes gradually became a real, living and breathing being in the eyes of the public for a number of reasons. The obvious place to start is with the sheer ingenuity of his creator. Arthur Conan Doyle was a cracking storyteller, coming up with characters and plots that amazed and delighted his publishers and his readers. The impecunious young doctor was keen to earn money from his writing and needed to appeal to a wide audience, so his style was simple and direct but never patronising. Everyone could enjoy the stories, from the enthusiastic child to the sophisticated adult.

The novels of Charles Dickens and many other authors of the time were serialised in monthly publications. But what if the reader missed a month's episode? In many instances, interest was lost in the story and further issues were not purchased. Conan Doyle recognised the wisdom of offering the reader a complete adventure in each issue of a magazine and suggested it to his publishers. Fortunately, the proprietors of *The Strand Magazine* agreed with this revolutionary philosophy, and Sherlock Holmes became the first literary character to appear in a continuing series.

Thanks to his regular scheduled appearances in *The Strand Magazine*, Sherlock Holmes very soon came to have a special place in his readers's lives, and in their homes. As with any new acquaintance, each meeting provided more information about his intriguing personality and his idiosyncratic lifestyle. In another masterly touch, the author provided just enough physical description to satisfy the reader and allow each individual to form in his or her own mind their own vision of Sherlock Holmes. Illustrators added to the picture that was forming, but it is fair to say that we all have our own interpretation of how Holmes looks and behaves, which is why we so often have strong feelings for or against a particular actor who has taken the role.

Crucially, Sherlock Holmes inhabited the same world as his readers. Much of the fiction of the time dealt with improbable romances, exotic locations or rarefied lifestyles. Holmes, however, walked the familiar streets and patronised the same shops, restaurants, theatres and concert halls frequented by his public. One wonders how many readers experienced a frisson at the notion that the tall young man just ahead of them in the queue at the Wigmore Street Post Office might be Sherlock Holmes... Even in the twenty-first century, much of Holmes's London is still tangible and we can continue to follow in his footsteps.

2

'A SINGULAR SET OF PEOPLE, WATSON'

WHEN ONE ENTERS THE world of Sherlock Holmes, one is almost inevitably drawn to the world of Sherlock Holmes enthusiasts. Initially known as Sherlockians in the United States and Holmesians in the UK, the terms are now pretty much interchangeable and used according to each individual's preference. Doyleans, on the other hand, have a more expanded interest in the life and other works of Arthur Conan Doyle, although one can easily be both a Sherlockian (or Holmesian) and a Doylean.

There are a number of misconceptions about Holmes aficionados. Many people, especially members of the media, think that we all:

- Go everywhere dressed in Victorian clothing
- Hold meetings that entirely revolve around murder mystery weekends

- Have long, boring conversations about every tiny detail in the stories
- Belong to secret societies that are incredibly difficult to join
- Actually believe that Sherlock Holmes was a real person
- Are generally a bunch of sad, lonely weirdos

In fact:

When the Sherlock Holmes Society of London makes its occasional trips to Switzerland, we do dress as characters from the stories. It's part of the experience and provides a great deal of amusement. There are also times when a few of us are requested to turn up in costume for special occasions, such as charity events or business launches, in order to generate publicity. Some of us are reasonably expert on Victorian and Edwardian attire and have provided assistance for museum exhibitions and dramatic productions. But most of the time we look like normal people.

- A few of our friends do run murder mystery events as a sideline. However, to our knowledge this is not anyone's sole source of entertainment.
- Most of the time we talk about almost everything except Sherlock Holmes. But, as with all literary societies, there always will be a few hard-headed scholars who need to learn to loosen up a bit. If one of the bores manages to corner you at a meeting, someone will swiftly come to your rescue before your eyes glaze over.

- There are hundreds of Sherlockian societies, nearly all of which are very easy to join. The one that maintains a degree of intrigue about it is the Baker Street Irregulars; one becomes a BSI by invitation only.

- Believe it or not, we do know that Sherlock Holmes was a creation of Sir Arthur Conan Doyle. The concept of pretending that Conan Doyle was Watson's literary agent and that Holmes was real is known as 'The Grand Game' amongst those who play it. There's more about this elsewhere in the book.

- We're actually a very sociable bunch and rather a lot of fun!

Anthony D. Howlett in character as Professor Moriarty, with the Reichenbach Falls behind him, on the Sherlock Holmes Society of London's 1991 Swiss pilgrimage. *Photo copyright Jean Upton*

There are hundreds of societies that encompass all ages, interests and walks of life. Several people of our acquaintance used to bring their toddlers to meetings; these toddlers have now grown into enthusiastic adult members of the societies. The recent annual dinner of the Sherlock Holmes Society of London, for example, was attended by several teenagers, a couple of nonagenarians and all ages in between. Members of the different societies to which we belong have included former US presidents, taxi drivers, librarians, doctors, lawyers, artists, actors, members of parliament, teachers, travel agents, armed forces personnel, science-fiction writers, police officers, used-car salesmen, students, computer programmers… the list just goes on and on. The important factor is that we all love Sherlock Holmes.

3

'THAT MIXTURE OF IMAGINATION AND REALITY'

• SHERLOCK HOLMES – FACT AND FICTION •

A NUMBER OF YEARS ago Anthony Howlett, then chairman of the Sherlock Holmes Society of London, was asked by a journalist: 'Was Sherlock Holmes a real person or a fictional character?' Tony's simple and direct answer was 'Yes.'

THE AUTHOR

Both fact and fiction start with Arthur Conan Doyle, physician and author, born on 22 May 1859 in Edinburgh, to Anglo-Irish parents. As a writer, he had some success with his early short stories, but his first attempt at a novel was rejected and he decided to try his hand at a mystery story. He said in his memoirs:

> Gaboriau had rather attracted me by the neat dovetailing of his plots, and Poe's masterful detective, M. Dupin, had from

boyhood been one of my heroes. But could I bring in an addition of my own? I thought of my old teacher Joe Bell, of his
eagle face, of his curious ways, of his eerie trick of spotting
details. If he were a detective, he would surely reduce this
fascinating but unorganised business to something nearer to
an exact science. I would try [to see] if I could get this effect.

His detective was to have been called Sherrinford Holmes, a
name soon altered to the neater and more forceful Sherlock
Holmes. He told a reporter: 'Years ago I made thirty runs against
a bowler by the name of Sherlock, and I always had a kindly
feeling for that name.' The surname was that of the American
essayist Oliver Wendell Holmes, also a physician, whom Conan
Doyle greatly admired. The narrator was originally called
Ormond Sacker, but fortunately that didn't last long.

The detective could not tell his own exploits, so he must
have a commonplace comrade as a foil – an educated man
of action, who could both join in the exploits and narrate
them. A drab, quiet name for this unostentatious man.
Watson would do…

And so Conan Doyle started work on the story he called 'A
Tangled Skein'. When it was complete he gave it a new title,
'A Study in Scarlet', and sent it out to the publishers. *The
Cornhill Magazine* found it too long for a short story and too
short for a novel. The firm of Arrowsmith kept the manuscript for three months and then returned it unread. Others
also rejected it. Finally came a letter from Ward Lock & Co.:

Dear Sir,

We have read your story and are pleased with it. We could not publish it this year, as the market is flooded at present with cheap fiction, but if you do not object to its being held over till next year we will give you £25 for the copyright.

Yours faithfully,

Ward Lock & Co.

October 30th 1886

Arthur Conan Doyle towards the beginning of his career as an author.
Collection of Roger Johnson and Jean Upton

Conan Doyle was not a rich man. After some hesitation, he accepted the offer, and the story became the leading item in *Beeton's Christmas Annual* for 1887. Ward Lock continued to publish the story in various editions until their copyright expired. Arthur Conan Doyle later said that he never received another penny for it.

British literature was enjoying a great vogue in the United States because the copyright laws there protected only American authors and works first published in America. The situation was hard on British writers whose work was freely pirated (one judge said that it must *not* be protected, because no true American could ever owe anything to a Britisher) but it did introduce much good literature to the American public.

In 1889, J.M. Stoddart came to London from Philadelphia to commission new works for *Lippincott's Monthly Magazine*. It says something for the success of his first book that Arthur Conan Doyle was one of three guests whom Stoddart invited to dinner at the Langham Hotel. The others were Thomas Patrick Gill MP and Oscar Wilde. Before the evening was over, Stoddart had commissioned a novel from each of the authors. From Wilde he got *The Picture of Dorian Gray*, and from Conan Doyle *The Sign of the Four*, the second exploit of Sherlock Holmes and Dr Watson.

Oscar Wilde was very complimentary about it, though he may not have realised that one of the principal characters, Thaddeus Sholto, had some of his own attributes, such as his taste for epigrams and his trick of speaking with a finger crooked across his mouth to hide his bad teeth.

Arthur Conan Doyle was then living in Southsea, but a fellow physician advised him to advance his career by specialising in London. He qualified in ophthalmology and put up his brass plate at 2 Upper Wimpole Street. Much later, he described the experience: 'For £120 a year, I got the use of a front room with part use of a waiting room. I was soon to find that they were both waiting rooms, and now I know that it was better so.'

No patients entered his consulting room, but he kept himself busy anyway. The early issues of *The Strand Magazine* had appeared, and he had begun writing more stories about Sherlock Holmes. As he explained:

Considering these various journals with their disconnected stories, it had struck me that a single character running through a series, if it only engaged the attention of the reader, would bind that reader to that particular magazine. On the other hand, it had long seemed to me that the ordinary serial might be an impediment rather than a help to a magazine since, sooner or later, one missed one number, and afterwards it had lost all interest. Clearly the ideal compromise was a character which carried through, and yet instalments which were complete in themselves. I believe that I was the first to realise this, and the Strand magazine the first to put it into practice.

From the first, the editor liked the stories. He commissioned the artist Sidney Paget to illustrate them, and it is in Paget's pictures that we first see the true Holmes portrayed.

It was almost entirely due to Arthur Conan Doyle and Sherlock Holmes that *The Strand Magazine* became by far the most popular periodical in Britain. The first twelve stories were immediately issued in book form as *The Adventures of Sherlock Holmes*. The writer was happy, the publisher was happy, and above all the public were happy. Without too much regret, Conan Doyle finally gave up the scalpel for the pen.

What of the man whom Conan Doyle called 'my old teacher, Joe Bell' – Dr Joseph Bell, who lectured at the medical school at Edinburgh University? An example of his technique, as recorded by a student, has a familiar ring:

'Well, my man, you've served in the army?'

'Aye, sir.'

'Not long discharged?'

'No, sir.'

'A Highland regiment?'

'Aye, sir.'

'A non-commissioned officer?'

'Aye, sir.'

'Stationed at Barbados?'

'Aye, sir.'

'You see, gentlemen, the man was a respectful man, but he did not remove his hat. They do not in the army, but he would have learned civilian ways had he been long discharged. He has an air of authority, and he is obviously Scottish. As to Barbados, his complaint is elephantiasis, which is West Indian, not British, and the Scottish regiments are at present in that particular island.'

Arthur Conan Doyle never hesitated to acknowledge that Dr Bell was the inspiration for Sherlock Holmes's methods, and Bell himself was proud of the association.

As he approached the last story, Conan Doyle began to wonder if he was doing the right thing. He wrote to his mother: 'I think of slaying Holmes and winding him up for good and all. He takes my mind from better things.'

But the old lady knew a good thing when she saw one. She persuaded him to write a further series. He demanded £1,000 for these new tales, in those days a breathtaking sum, and the

Dr Joseph Bell in deerstalker and Inverness. Can anyone doubt his influence?
Collection of Roger Johnson and Jean Upton

publishers agreed instantly. Even so, in the last of these adventures Holmes and the master criminal Professor Moriarty were sent plunging over the Reichenbach Falls, to lie for all time in 'that dreadful cauldron of swirling water and seething foam'.

Conan Doyle definitely intended to kill Sherlock Holmes – and yet, in devising a suitably dramatic death, he chose one that would not require the body to be produced. This was something for which the public, and even Conan Doyle himself, were at last to be profoundly grateful.

It is said that when 'The Final Problem' was published in December 1893, members of the public wore mourning bands on their sleeves. Certainly letters of protest were written to author and publisher. In his memoirs, Conan Doyle gleefully quotes one, from a lady, which bluntly commenced: 'You brute!'

Six years later, William Gillette became the living embodiment of the detective in his play *Sherlock Holmes: A Drama in Four Acts*, but there was nothing more from Conan Doyle, who was happily concentrating on the historical novels that he thought of as his important work.

Then in 1901, a friend, Bertram Fletcher Robinson, recounted the dramatic legend of a spectral hound that stalked Dartmoor by night. It was ideal material for a thrilling novel, and for the protagonist Conan Doyle naturally turned to the late Sherlock Holmes. The resulting story, *The Hound of the Baskervilles*, is the best known of all the detective's adventures, but it was made clear that this was a posthumous narrative of a case that had occurred before the terrible Reichenbach affair.

The novel was hugely popular. The world was ready for more Sherlock Holmes, as the international success of

William Gillette's play suggested, but what persuaded Conan Doyle was a publisher's offer of over £10,000 for a new series of adventures. To his mother he wrote: 'You will find that Holmes was never dead, and that he is now very much alive.'

Collier's Magazine published 'The Adventure of the Empty House' in September 1903. In London, where it appeared almost simultaneously in the *Strand*, an eyewitness said: 'The scenes at the railway bookstalls were worse than anything I ever saw at a bargain sale.'

The truth was out at last. Holmes had not died at Reichenbach. Using his knowledge of the Japanese martial arts, he had turned his enemy's strength against him, and sent the master criminal plunging into the depths alone. Since then, Holmes had pursued his fight against crime, unknown and unrecognised for some three years.

And now he was back in London. The stories continued to appear, but at intervals, because of Conan Doyle's other work. Besides the historical novels, he was writing plays, poems, war histories and science fiction. He became a field surgeon in the thick of the South African war, successfully adopted the causes of at least three people who had been wrongly convicted of crime, raised a local defence squad during the First World War and – to him most importantly – became the world's leading advocate of Spiritualism.

There were three more volumes of Sherlock Holmes stories: *The Valley of Fear*, a novel that combines a tantalising detective story and a riveting thriller; *His Last Bow*; and finally *The Casebook of Sherlock Holmes*, published in 1927.

Three years later, Arthur Conan Doyle died at the age of 71. On his gravestone are carved the words: 'Steel True, Blade Straight'. The same epitaph would serve for Sherlock Holmes, and when we come down to it, of course, Arthur Conan Doyle *was* Sherlock Holmes.

Except that by now Sherlock Holmes had a life of his own.

THE CHARACTER

Holmes was born in or about the year 1854 to an undistinguished family of country squires, but had inherited an artistic streak from his grandmother: 'a sister of Vernet, the French artist.' Holmes believed that this accounted for his own peculiar talents, which his elder brother Mycroft possessed to an even greater degree. On first mentioning him, in the case of 'The Greek Interpreter', Sherlock said:

If the art of the detective began and ended in reasoning from an armchair, my brother would be the greatest criminal agent that ever lived. But he has no ambition and no energy. He will not even go out of his way to verify his own solutions, and would rather be considered wrong than take the trouble to prove himself right. Again and again I have taken a problem to him, and have received an explanation which has afterwards proved to be the correct one. And yet he was absolutely incapable of working out the practical points which must be gone into before a case could be laid before a judge or jury.

This unambitious man entered the Civil Service, as an auditor. At least, that's what Sherlock Holmes first told Dr Watson. Much later, in reference to 'The Bruce-Partington Plans', he said:

> You are right in thinking that he is under the British government. You would also be right in a sense if you said that occasionally he *is* the British government. His position is unique. There has never been anything like it before, nor will be again. He has the tidiest and most orderly brain, with the greatest capacity for storing facts, of any man living. The same great powers which I have turned to the detection of crime he has used for this particular business. The conclusions of every department are passed to him, and he is the central exchange, the clearing-house, which makes out the balance. All other men are specialists, but his specialism is omniscience. Again and again his word has decided the national policy.

The respectful but distant adult relationship of the brothers suggests an equally curious upbringing, but we actually know nothing of those early years. For us, the story really begins at Sherlock's university – undoubtedly either Oxford or Cambridge – where the curious case of the *Gloria Scott* persuaded him that he might be able to turn his hobby into a profession. Leaving the university, he took lodgings in Montague Street, near the British Museum, for he was still studying. He aimed to become, not just another private detective, but the world's first private consulting detective. In *A Study in Scarlet* we read:

> Here in London we have lots of government detectives and
> lots of private ones. When these fellows are at fault they come
> to me, and I manage to put them on the right scent. They lay
> all the evidence before me, and I am generally able, by the help
> of my knowledge of the history of crime, to set them straight.

Slowly he built up a network of contacts and a reputation.
What he needed next, though he may not have realised it, was
a chronicler.

In 1878, John H. Watson had gone straight from medical
school to train as an army surgeon, and shortly found himself
in India, where the Second Afghan War was raging. Severely
wounded at the Battle of Maiwand, he was invalided home as
soon as possible, to live as best he could on £11 6d a day.

Learning of his search for cheaper lodgings, an old
acquaintance from St Bartholomew's Hospital told him of
Sherlock Holmes, who had found a nice flat in Baker Street
and needed someone to share with him. The doctor and the
detective met for the first time in the chemical laboratory at
Bart's hospital. The meeting is recorded in *A Study in Scarlet*:

> 'Dr. Watson, Mr. Sherlock Holmes,' said Stamford, intro-
> ducing us.
>   'How are you?' he said cordially, gripping my hand with
> a strength for which I should hardly have given him credit.
> 'You have been in Afghanistan, I perceive.'
>   'How on earth did you know that?' I asked in astonishment.
>   'Never mind,' said he, chuckling to himself. 'The ques-
> tion now is about haemoglobin...'

At once they established their true roles: as master and disciple. Holmes's deduction was of no consequence to him, but it bewildered Watson, as it bewilders us.

Later, when they were comfortably settled into their rooms at No. 221B, Holmes explained:

> The train of reasoning ran: Here is a gentleman of a medical type but with the air of a military man. Clearly an army doctor, then. He has just come from the tropics, for his face is dark, and that is not the natural tint of his skin, for his wrists are fair. He has undergone hardship and sickness, as his haggard face says clearly. His left arm has been injured. He holds it in a stiff and unnatural manner. Where in the tropics could an English army doctor have seen such hardship and got his arm wounded? Clearly in Afghanistan.

Watson, meaning it as a compliment, replied: 'You remind me of Edgar Allan Poe's Dupin.' Holmes, however, wasn't impressed: 'Now, in my opinion, Dupin was a very inferior fellow... He had some analytical genius, no doubt; but he was by no means such a phenomenon as Poe appeared to imagine.' Watson thought: 'This fellow may be very clever... but he is certainly very conceited.'

The young Holmes was very ambitious, and the comparison with Dupin seems to have touched a nerve. The two were more alike than he admitted, not least in their attitude to the police.

The first official detectives Watson meets are Gregson and Lestrade, whom Holmes described as 'quick and energetic, but conventional – shockingly so.' Being out of their depth, he says, is their normal state.

Sherlock Holmes had found his biographer, and Dr Watson had found his life's work.

<hr />

For nearly eight years, Holmes and Watson shared the rooms in Baker Street. They shared adventures too. Then in July 1888 came another turning point, when a young lady arrived at 221B to present to them the problem of *The Sign of the Four*. Her name was Mary Morstan, and she brought with her murder, conspiracy, betrayal, oriental treasure – and romance. John Watson fell deeply in love with her, and even Holmes, though 'he never spoke of the softer passions save with a gibe and a sneer', considered her 'one of the most charming young ladies I ever met'. For John and Mary, the adventure ended most happily. And for Holmes?

'The division seems rather unfair,' I remarked. 'You have done all the work in this business. I get a wife out of it. Jones gets all the credit. Pray, what remains for you?'

'For me,' said Sherlock Holmes, 'there still remains the cocaine-bottle.'

Holmes's drug taking was an unwise and dangerous practice, but it was not illegal then, and we know that in time Watson was able to wean him off it.

So Watson took a wife and left the Baker Street household. He and Holmes saw each other irregularly after that.

Occasionally Watson would call at Baker Street, often to find himself involved in a case, such as 'The Blue Carbuncle' or 'A Scandal in Bohemia'. It was in the course of this latter adventure that Sherlock Holmes was defeated by a woman, the beautiful opera singer Irene Adler, former mistress of the King of Bohemia.

> To Sherlock Holmes [said Watson] she is always THE woman. I have seldom heard him mention her under any other name. In his eyes she eclipses and predominates the whole of her sex. It was not that he felt any emotion akin to love for Irene Adler. All emotions, and that one particularly, were abhorrent to his cold, precise but admirably balanced mind.

Many romantically inclined persons have insisted that the detective nursed a life-long passion for the diva; some even claim that they became lovers. But Watson, down-to-earth, reliable Watson, makes it quite clear that such things were simply not in Holmes's nature.

⸎

Now and again Holmes would call upon Watson to enlist his help in such cases as 'The Crooked Man' or 'The Boscombe Valley Mystery'. Life continued, but Holmes was continually aware of a malevolent organising genius who was ultimately responsible for half that was evil and nearly all that was undetected in London. His name was ex-Professor James Moriarty, and Holmes called him the Napoleon of Crime.

In the spring of 1891, Holmes slipped quietly into Watson's house. The net was already tightening around Moriarty's gang. Holmes planned to go abroad for a few days, to give the police a free hand, and for old times' sake he asked Watson to go with him. When they reached Strasbourg, however, there was grave news from Scotland Yard: the gang had indeed been captured, but without its leader. Moriarty had followed Sherlock Holmes to Europe and was out for revenge.

In 'The Final Problem' you can read how Watson was lured away, leaving his friend alone at the great Falls of Reichenbach, and how he returned to find, as he supposed, that both the master criminal and the master detective had perished, their bodies lost forever in that dreadful swirling, booming cauldron. Sick at heart, he returned to London, to his wife and his medical practice. From time to time he tried his hand at detective work, but without much success.

Holmes had survived, and had gone travelling. He spent two years in Tibet, then passed through Persia, looked in at Mecca, paid a brief visit to Khartoum, and then, at last, to France.

The call of London was strong however. After three years, the wanderer returned, to find that his friend had suffered a grievous loss: poor Mary, her health never over-strong, had died. Watson, of course, was overjoyed to see Holmes again, and the partnership was resumed with the pursuit and capture of Moriarty's right-hand man, Colonel Sebastian Moran. Sherlock Holmes was free once more to devote his life to examining those interesting little problems that the complex life of London presents so plentifully.

Clients came once more to 221B. Now, perhaps because Holmes felt secure in himself, his attitude to the police became less arrogant. 'There may be an occasional want of imaginative intuition at Scotland Yard,' he said, 'but they lead the world for thoroughness and method.' The appreciation was mutual; at the successful conclusion of a late case, 'The Six Napoleons', Lestrade told him:

I've seen you handle a good many cases, Mr. Holmes, but I don't know that I ever knew a more workmanlike one than that. We're not jealous of you at Scotland Yard. No, sir, we are very proud of you, and if you come down tomorrow, there's not a man, from the oldest inspector to the youngest constable, who wouldn't be glad to shake you by the hand.

But a new century was dawning, and perhaps Watson at least was beginning to feel his age. In 1902 he left Baker Street to set up a practice in Queen Anne Street, and shortly afterwards he married again. The following year, at the age of 49, Sherlock Holmes retired, leaving Baker Street forever. With his usual talent for the unexpected, he turned from detecting crime in London to keeping bees on the Sussex Downs.

He and Watson saw little of each other, and he refused all offers to take up his detective practice again. He broke his retirement only when it became clear that war was coming, and even then it took a personal visit from the prime minister to persuade him to infiltrate and break a German spy ring. The climax came on 2 August 1914, the most terrible Aug in the history of the world. It's good to know that John H. Watson was in at the end.

Our last sight is of the two friends looking out over the dark North Sea and the lights of Harwich. The master spy has been arrested, but war is inevitable.

'There's an east wind coming, Watson.'

'I think not, Holmes. It is very warm.'

'Good old Watson! You are the one fixed point in a changing age. There's an east wind coming all the same, such a wind as never blew on England yet. It will be cold and bitter, Watson, and a good many of us may wither before its blast. But it's God's own wind none the less, and a cleaner, better, stronger land will lie in the sunshine when the storm has cleared.'

That final exchange is as typical of both men as the first one was, all those years ago in the chemical laboratory at Bart's Hospital.

No doubt Sherlock Holmes was engaged in intelligence work for the duration of the war, and no doubt he returned in 1918 to his bee farm. He may still be there. At all events, we may be sure that he is still alive, for his obituary has yet to appear in *The Times*. Besides, he is immortal, and immortals cannot die.

4

'YOUR PICTURES ARE NOT UNLIKE YOU'

• THE ILLUSTRATORS •

IN *A STUDY IN SCARLET*, Dr Watson provides his first description of the appearance of Sherlock Holmes:

His very person and appearance were such as to strike the attention of the most casual observer. In height he was rather over six feet, and so excessively lean that he seemed to be considerably taller. His eyes were sharp and piercing, save during those intervals of torpor to which I have alluded; and his thin, hawk-like nose gave his whole expression an air of alertness and decision. His chin, too, had the prominence and squareness which mark the man of determination. His hands were invariably blotted with ink and stained with chemicals, yet he was possessed of extraordinary delicacy of touch, as I frequently had occasion to observe when I watched him manipulating his fragile philosophical instruments.

D.H. Friston's several illustrations for Holmes's initial appearance in *Beeton's Christmas Annual* of 1887 provided only one displaying Holmes's face. He is shown in profile, inspecting the word 'Rache', written in blood at the scene of the murder. Holmes is indeed taller than the other characters, clean shaven but with impressive sideburns, and does have a hawk-like nose as described in the text. However, his excessive leanness is not readily apparent. Interestingly, he is shown wearing a rather bulky Inverness cloak with its distinctive short cape covering the shoulders; a costume detail that has been retained by later illustrators. Fortunately, they did not choose to do the same with Lestrade's alarmingly snug trousers!

When *A Study in Scarlet* was reprinted in 1888 by Ward, Lock & Co. the illustrations were by Conan Doyle's own father, Charles, who in his younger days was an accomplished artist. Like the Holmes family, the Doyles had art in their blood. In his autobiography *Memories and Adventures*, Conan Doyle relates:

My grandfather was a widower with a numerous family, of which four boys and one girl survived. Each of the boys made a name for himself, for all inherited the artistic powers of their father. The elder, James Doyle, wrote The Chronicles of England, illustrated with coloured pictures by himself … Another brother was Henry Doyle, a great judge of old paintings, and in later years the manager of the National Gallery in Dublin, where he earned his CB. The third son was Richard Doyle, whose whimsical humour made him famous in Punch, the cover of which with its dancing elves is still so familiar an object. Finally came Charles Doyle, my father.

Unfortunately, in his later life Charles Doyle suffered from alcoholism, epilepsy and other ailments, and his illustrations for his son's book are sadly crude. He seems to have taken little notice of the text, for he gives Holmes a full beard and a noticeably small nose. At the murder scene, Watson's horrified reaction is almost comical, and Lestrade looks disconcertingly smug.

Arthur cannot have been entirely happy with his father's illustrations, but in his memoirs he loyally defended Charles Doyle's reputation:

His painting was done spasmodically and the family did not always reap the benefit, for Edinburgh is full of water-colours which he had given away. It is one of my unfulfilled schemes to collect as many as possible and to have a Charles Doyle exhibition in London, for the critics would be surprised to find what a great and original artist he was – far the greatest, in my opinion, of the family. His brush was concerned not only with fairies and delicate themes of the kind, but with wild and fearsome subjects, so that his work had a very peculiar style of its own, mitigated by great natural humour. He was more terrible than Blake and less morbid than Wiertz. His originality is best shown by the fact that one hardly knows with whom to compare him. In prosaic Scotland, however, he excited wonder rather than admiration, and he was only known in the larger world of London by pen-and-ink book illustrations which were not his best mode of expression.

sort of little Kangaroo rat. He is our Grand-daddy – bless him!

The Lias. Consists as a rule of bluish clay. Is found right across Cyland from Yorkshire to Devon. The inhabitants were mostly reptiles and do not appear to have been a more pleasant crowd than the Trias contains. Already many of the existing shells &c were to be found. I do not think that the Mammal had caught on much as yet. If you come to think of it the Kangaroo Rat would have a poor time in a world of crocodiles.

Perilous Position of our Grand-dad.

Page from *A Synopsis of Geology*, written by Conan Doyle for his second wife, Jean Leckie. The cartoon shows the 'Perilous position of our grand-dad' described in the text as 'a sort of little kangaroo rat. He is our grand-daddy – bless him!' *Collection of Roger Johnson and Jean Upton*

Arthur also dabbled in pen-and-ink drawings, mainly cartoons representing different stages of his career and observations during his many travels. Most famously 'The Old Horse', drawn towards the end of his life, shows an elderly carthorse (himself) towing a wagon piled high with packages that are labelled with the significant activities and achievements of his lifetime. The caption reads: 'The Old Horse has pulled a heavy load a long way, but he is well cared for and with six weeks able and six months grass he will be on the road once more.'

In 1891 George Hutchinson illustrated yet another edition *Study in Scarlet*, and his drawings of Holmes, Watson and the rest are much more faithful to the author's descriptions. He also shows us something of the sitting room at 221B.

Sidney Paget was the artist who had the greatest impact however. In his illustrations for *The Strand Magazine*, the image of Holmes and Watson became iconic. Paget's family too had art in the blood: three of the five brothers – Henry, Walter and Sidney – were artists and illustrators. The commission to illustrate the Sherlock Holmes stories was actually intended for Walter Paget but, through some misunderstanding, Sidney got the job. It is popularly thought that he used Walter as the model for Holmes, and although the family denied the claim, Arthur Conan Doyle evidently believed it. He said in *Memories and Adventures*:

> Before I leave the subject of the many impersonations of Holmes I may say that all of them, and all the drawings, are very unlike my own original idea of the man. I saw him as very tall – 'over 6 feet, but so excessively lean that he seemed considerably taller,' said A Study in Scarlet. He had, as I imagined him, a thin razor-like face, with a great hawks-bill of a nose, and two small eyes, set close together on either side of it. Such was my conception. It chanced, however, that poor Sidney Paget who, before his premature death, drew all the original pictures, had a younger brother whose name, I think, was Walter, who served him as a model. The handsome Walter took the place of the more powerful but uglier Sherlock, and perhaps from the point of view of my lady readers it was as well. The stage has followed the type set up by the pictures.

Paget used many of his own possessions as inspiration for details in the illustrations. Photographs exist of him wearing a deerstalker, which he introduced as Holmes's headgear in 'The Boscombe Valley Mystery' in 1891, and it is eventually shown mid-flight into the Reichenbach Falls while Holmes and Moriarty grapple on the slippery ledge. It did not, however, share the arch criminal's watery grave, as a letter from Winifred Paget to *Picture Post* revealed on 16 December 1950:

> Many years after my father's death, at the early age of forty-seven, the deerstalker was savagely attacked by moths who apparently are no respecters of ancient relics and reluctantly my mother consigned it to the dustbin, so I fear there is an empty peg beside that on which one hopes Watson's bowler still hangs on 221B Baker Street, unless, this too has suffered the same fate!

In 1951 Sidney Paget's own basket chair, which appears in his pictures of the living quarters at 221B, was among the items generously contributed by his family to the 1951 Sherlock Holmes exhibition in Baker Street. In all, Paget produced 356 published Sherlock Holmes illustrations for *The Strand Magazine*. When he died in 1908, his brother Walter stepped in to illustrate one story, 'The Dying Detective'. The results of Sidney Paget's work, as seen in *The Strand*, were often at the mercy of the engravers: some were better than others. When one has the opportunity to view them, his original watercolours are often far superior to what ended up on the printed page. In any case, Paget's impact in Sherlockian lore

'A Retrospection' – an original watercolour illustration by Sidney Paget for *The Hound of the Baskervilles*. *Courtesy of Mary Ann Bradley and Michael Whelan*

is so strong that when Granada television made its series with Jeremy Brett in the 1980s, the appearance of many characters, costumes and sets attempted to replicate Paget's illustrations as closely as possible.

The first two stories published after Paget's untimely death were graced with excellent illustrations by Arthur Twidle, who had already provided a series of very fine pictures for the Conan Doyle Author's Edition of the stories in 1903. Unfortunately he fell out with the art editor, and drew no more for *The Strand Magazine*. Other popular artists of the period contributed their interpretations to *The Strand*, including Gilbert Holiday, H.M. Brock, Joseph Simpson, Alec Ball, A. Gilbert, Howard Elcock, and – the best in many ways – Frank Wiles.

Frank Wiles made a particular visual impact with his incisive full-colour portrait of the detective on the cover of the September 1914 issue, containing the first instalment of *The Valley of Fear*. His Holmes, though recognisably based on Paget's interpretation, is closer to Conan Doyle's specifications, with a lean face, strong chin, intent expression and sharply angled cheekbones.

England had Sidney Paget, but the United States had Frederic Dorr Steele, whose elegantly simple, strong lines provided the arresting covers and illustrations for *Collier's Magazine*. This was the Holmes that inhabited the imagination of turn-of-the-century Americans. Steele had the advantage of a living, recognisable model, in this case the actor William Gillette, whose presence on stage as the Great Detective was by now world famous. Lithe, graceful and powerful, Steele's Holmes has a commanding presence on the page whether in dressing gown or in tweeds. The colour illustrations are lessons in the beauty of simple draughtsmanship; not a line is wasted nor does any colour overwhelm the overall effect. The black-and-white drawings, carried out in charcoal pencil, are

Collier's Magazine cover illustration by Frederic Dorr Steele, using William Gillette as his model. *Collection of Roger Johnson and Jean Upton*

strong, energetic and moody. Steele was a perfectionist, and it was not unusual for him to do a literal cut and paste, chopping and changing elements until he was content with the final result. He and Gillette formed a lasting friendship and both attended dinners of the Baker Street Irregulars (BSI).

Some of Steele's illustrations show Holmes with the curved pipe that Gillette had introduced, thus adding another element, along with Paget's deerstalker, to the long-standing established image of Sherlock Holmes.

───◦⊙◦───

It is impossible to cover all of the illustrators, especially since the list continues to grow with each passing year. There are, however, several within the world of Sherlockian publications who deserve mention.

Julian Wolff, who became head of the Baker Street Irregulars in 1960, created an attractive and imaginative series of maps of canonical locations, some of which originally appeared in Edgar W. Smith's *Baker Street and Beyond*, others in *The Baker Street Journal*. In 1984 they were collected and printed as *The Sherlockian Atlas*. They depict London, England, Europe, the United States, Dartmoor and other significant sites, including a layout of the interior of 221B Baker Street. In the 1960s Wolff also hand-coloured a set for Lord Donegall, editor of *The Sherlock Holmes Journal*, who had them printed as Christmas cards. These cards are now highly collectible, as are the original maps.

Henry Lauritzen, a professional artist and cartoonist, was president of the Danish Baker Street Irregulars in the 1970s. For many years he provided affectionate and witty drawings for numerous Sherlockian publications, including *The Baker Street Journal*. His artwork can be found in the Baker Street Irregulars's international series publication, *Scandinavia and Sherlock Holmes*.

Since 1983, Scott Bond, an art director and designer, has provided the popular and amusing *Art in the Blood* cartoon for each issue of *The Baker Street Journal*. He also designs the creative pictorial menu for the annual dinner of the Baker Street Irregulars. His specially designed Christmas cards, usually providing an arts and crafts project for the more ambitious recipients, are eagerly awaited every year. Scott has designed a number of Sherlockian collectibles, including scion pins and an attractive enamelled tin that reposes in our own collection.

One of Scott Bond's interpretations of Sherlock Holmes. This drawing from 1981 predates his 'Art in the Blood' series for *The Baker Street Journal*. *Courtesy of Scott Bond*

Jeff Decker, an artist and prodigious caricaturist, has graced the pages of *The Baker Street Journal* with his gloriously eccentric *Tales From Dartmoor* cartoons. He illustrated numerous Sherlockian books and journals, as well as designing Christmas cards for some of his devoted fans. Jeff also established a reputation for creating imaginative pictorial representations of investitures, on request, for various members of the Baker Street Irregulars.

Jean-Pierre Cagnat is a cartoonist and illustrator for *Le Monde*. His extremely perceptive and often hilariously grotesque artwork has also appeared in *National Geographic*, *Marie Claire*, *Reader's Digest* and numerous other international publications as well as those of a Sherlockian theme. Jean-Pierre is co-founder of the Sherlock Holmes Society of France and in 2001 published *It is Always a Joy... Around the World of*

Tales from Dartmoor

Jeff Decker's 'Tales from Dartmoor' in *The Baker Street Journal* reveals the truth behind the Hound of the Baskervilles. *Courtesy of Jeff Decker and Steven Rothman*

Sherlock Holmes in Fifteen Years, chronicling his travels and the Sherlockians that he met along the way.

Philip Cornell is 'Expedition Artist' and vice-president of the Sydney Passengers, based in New South Wales, Australia. A remarkably versatile artist with a delightfully crazy wit, Phil provides cartoons, caricatures and illustrations for the society's journal, *The Passengers' Log*, and has recently branched out into the world of graphic novels.

COMIC BOOKS AND GRAPHIC NOVELS

Almost from the beginning, cartoons featuring Sherlock Holmes or something very like him have appeared in numerous magazines and newspapers. The earliest strip cartoon was *Chubblock Holmes*, created in 1893 by Jack Butler Yeats, brother of the poet William Butler Yeats, for *Comic Cuts*. In the United States *Padlock Bones* appeared in 1904 in William Randolph Hearst's daily newspapers. Other early contributions to the genre were *Sherlocko the Monk*, *Sherlock Guck* and *Shylock Bones*. Holmes-like characters also appeared in *Thimble Theatre* (featuring Popeye), *Mutt and Jeff* and *Hairbreadth Harry*. The move into comic books was no great leap.

Classics Illustrated (originally *Classic Comics*) was beloved of pupils who didn't want to have to knuckle down and read an entire novel. Why bother, when it was available in comic book form? Enough plot and dialogue was provided to fob off one's parents and teachers – at least temporarily. The '3 Famous Mysteries' issue, published in 1944, was a bumper edition, including 'The Sign of the 4' (*sic*), Edgar Allan Poe's 'The Murders in the Rue Morgue' and Guy de Maupassant's 'The Flayed Hand'. Perhaps in order to ensure its appeal to young male readers, the romance is left out of this adaptation, as Watson is portrayed as white-haired and bespectacled; obviously too old for Mary Morstan.

The Adventures of Sherlock Holmes, published in 1947, has an appealingly lurid cover showing a matinée-idol Holmes, complete with dressing gown, pipe and violin, apparently contemplating the slavering Hound of the Baskervilles, while a gory hand inscribes 'Rache'. Despite the promises of the cover design and title, the only story contained within is *The Hound*.

In 1986 Renegade Press began its series, entitled *Cases of Sherlock Holmes*, with stylish black-and-white illustrations by Dan Day, which were modelled on Basil Rathbone and Nigel Bruce.

In 1988 *Eternity* compiled the classic *Sherlock Holmes* comic strip from the 1950s and began to issue them in monthly instalments. Written by Edith Meiser, better known for her radio adaptations, with artwork by Frank Giacoia, the adventures were originally printed in daily newspaper instalments and were renowned for their accurate portrayals of the original stories.

Other comic book publishers have added their own versions of Sherlock Holmes to this literary niche, even going so far as to partner him with superheroes.

Considered by some as merely comic books for adults, graphic novels go beyond the concept of playful cartoon storytelling; the mood is often much darker and more dangerous. An art form in itself, the graphic novel attracts high-quality artists and writers who enjoy the opportunity to flex their creative muscles. Amongst the most highly regarded are the four Sherlock Holmes novels published by SelfMadeHero, adapted by Ian Edginton and illustrated by I.N.J. Culbard. A particular favourite of ours is *Sherlock Holmes: The Painful Predicament of Alice Faulkner*, adapted from William Gillette's play and illustrated in a strikingly moody fashion by Bret M. Herholz.

There have been many interpretations of Sherlock Holmes in this format, and undoubtedly more will follow. Some stick to the Conan Doyle stories, others go off on a bit of a tangent. Just have a look in specialist shops or on the internet. Sherlock Holmes and zombies? Believe it!

5

'IT MAY HAVE BEEN A COMEDY, OR IT MAY HAVE BEEN A TRAGEDY'

• HOLMES ON STAGE •

BY 1893, THANKS TO *The Strand Magazine*, Sherlock Holmes was already, in the public mind, the ultimate detective. He made his stage début that year at the Royal Court, in a satirical revue called *Under the Clock*, written and performed by Charles Brookfield and Seymour Hicks. It was a taste of things to come – some things, anyway, as Holmes and Watson have served as targets for parody and weapons for satire ever since. They first appeared in a straight play the following year, though it was notably less successful: *Sherlock Holmes* by Charles Rogers ran for just six performances at the Theatre Royal, Glasgow.

Arthur Conan Doyle had no hand in either production, and gained nothing from them. As far as he was concerned, Holmes was dead. But in 1897 he turned his mind to

writing his own play about the detective. When it was complete, he sent it to the leading actors of the day: Sir Henry
Irving, who was not interested, and H. Beerbohm Tree, who
demanded more changes than the author would accept.
Eventually the script went to William Gillette, an American
actor who had enjoyed great success in his own plays. With
Conan Doyle's permission, he adapted – or rather, rewrote
– *Sherlock Holmes*. To his enquiry, 'May I marry Holmes?' the
famous reply was, 'You may marry or murder or do what
you like with him.'

The critics were not always kind, but *Sherlock Holmes* by
Arthur Conan Doyle and William Gillette was popular with
audiences from its first performance in Buffalo, New York,
in October 1899. When Gillette brought the play to England
two years later, it was an established hit. Part of the success
was down to Gillette's own performance: in America, for
more than a generation, he became the definitive Holmes,
and his is the image that we see in the classic illustrations of
Frederic Dorr Steele. Conan Doyle told him: 'You made the
poor hero of the anaemic printed page a very limp object as
compared with the glamour of your own personality which
you infuse into his stage presentment.' But the play was popular even without him. While he was performing in England,
Cuyler Hastings toured as Sherlock Holmes in America and
then in Australia. When Gillette returned home, companies led by Julian Royce, H.A. Saintsbury and H. Hamilton
Stewart took the play around the United Kingdom.

Sherlock Holmes remained in Gillette's repertoire for
more than thirty years. In 1929, when he began his farewell

William Gillette in his most famous role. *Collection of Roger Johnson and Jean Upton*

tour, the novelist Booth Tarkington said: 'I would rather see you play Sherlock Holmes than be a child again on Christmas morning.'

Without Gillette, the play began to be thought of as old-fashioned. Despite the occasional performance, interest waned until 1974, when the Royal Shakespeare Company staged the first West End production of *Sherlock Holmes* in nearly seventy years. The director, Frank Dunlop, recognised that good melodrama should be played with complete sincerity. His cast, headed by John Wood and Philip Locke as Holmes and Moriarty, gave as much to Gillette's text as they did to

Shakespeare, and the result was stunning. After a triumphant eight months, the company took *Sherlock Holmes* to America, where it played for more than a year, with some changes of cast: John Wood's successors included John Neville, Robert Stephens and Leonard Nimoy.

----◦◦◦◦----

It would be impossible to list every Sherlock Holmes play that has been put on in Britain, and the effort would be pointless anyway. However, there are plays and productions that seem to us to be significant.

In 1910 Arthur Conan Doyle found himself with a six-month lease on the Adelphi Theatre after the rapid failure of *The House of Temperley*, a play based on his own novel *Rodney Stone*. As a replacement he dramatised one of the most gothic of the Sherlock Holmes stories, *The Speckled Band*. H.A. Saintsbury, already used to the character, was cast as Holmes, with Lyn Harding magnificent as the villainous Dr Grimesby Rylott ('Roylott' in the original). The production achieved a very respectable run, though it was less successful in America. The play is occasionally revived.

Conan Doyle had another try in 1921, with *The Crown Diamond*, which uses some elements from the story 'The Empty House'. There were just twenty-eight performances in all, with Dennis Neilson-Terry as Holmes, and the play has, we think, never been staged again. The author did salvage something from the wreckage: *The Crown Diamond* was adapted as 'The Mazarin Stone', widely considered one of the worst of the short stories.

The year 1923 saw *The Return of Sherlock Holmes*, written by J.E.H. Terry & J. Arthur Rose as a vehicle for Eille Norwood, who had enjoyed great success as Holmes in a long series of silent films. The complicated plot draws on several of the original stories, but somehow the authors managed to keep it under control. The play in general was well received, and Norwood's performance, which took advantage of his genius for disguise, was highly praised.

The last pre-war play of much consequence was *The Holmeses of Baker Street* by Basil Mitchell, which had a short run in the West End in 1933. The main character is actually Shirley Holmes, who has inherited her widowed father's talent for observation and deduction, much to his dismay. *The Times* called Felix Aylmer's portrayal of the elderly Sherlock 'a flawless piece of acting', though Nigel Playfair's broadly comic performance as Watson was less well received. The play was adapted for American audiences, but was generally considered dull.

The year 1953 brought major but contrasting productions on both sides of the Atlantic. Early in the year the Sadler's Wells Ballet presented *The Great Detective*, choreographed by Margaret Dale to music by Richard Arnell. *The Times* noted that the story is 'more bizarre than Mr. Holmes's most fervent admirers will credit'. Kenneth Macmillan portrayed both the detective and the professor, and Stanley Holden was the doctor. Arnell's delightful music has been released on record more than once, but the ballet itself, though evidently entertaining, has not been staged since.

In America, Basil Rathbone, still being typecast seven years after his last appearance in the role, had given in, and commissioned his wife Ouida Bergere to write a Sherlock Holmes play for him. The result, alas, was over-long, over-wordy and over-complicated. No producer was interested, and *Sherlock Holmes* ended up with Bill Doll, a press agent with no experience of production. Despite a good cast and a competent director, the three-week try-out in Boston was tepidly received. You might have thought that, when it opened in New York, people who remembered the films and the radio plays would be keen to see Basil Rathbone in person, but in fact the audiences stayed away. *Sherlock Holmes* closed after three performances. It was all very sad.

In the early 1960s, inspired perhaps by the success of *My Fair Lady*, Jerome Coopersmith thought that the time had come for a Sherlock Holmes musical. With songs by Raymond Jessel and Marion Grudeff (and, uncredited, Sheldon Harnick and Jerry Bock) *Baker Street* may not have matched Lerner and Loewe's masterpiece, but it ran for nearly a year on Broadway, and the original cast album was a hit. The lyrics match the wit of Coopersmith's script, and the actors did well by them. Fritz Weaver was an impressive Holmes, with Peter Sallis as Watson – whose position as the detective's associate was partly usurped by Irene Adler (Inga Swenson).

Sherlock's Last Case by Matthew Lang, first produced at the Open Space in London in 1974, was a truly bitter comedy, inspired by the films of Basil Rathbone and Nigel Bruce. The depiction of a downtrodden Dr Watson (Peter Bayliss) finally taking a gruesome revenge for his years of mistreatment by the vain, arrogant detective (Julian Glover) attracted mixed reviews. Ten years later a revised version was presented in

Los Angeles, and Matthew Lang's true identity was revealed. *Sherlock's Last Case* was actually written by Charles Marowitz. In 1987 the play reached Broadway, with Frank Langella and Donal Donnelly as Holmes and Watson. As before, the critics were divided, but there have been a dozen or more productions since.

In the 1970s *The Hound of the Baskervilles* became a popular subject for the stage, despite the practical problems of presenting a truly impressive canine monster. Tim Kelly's version, first produced in California in 1976, quickly became a staple for amateur theatre groups on both sides of the ocean, though there seems to be no obvious reason why this particular *Hound* should be more popular than the others.

More imaginative is *The Crucifer of Blood* by Paul Giovanni, adapted, with some audacious variations, from *The Sign of Four*. On Broadway in 1978, Paxton Whitehead as Holmes and Glenn Close as Irene St Clair were especially commended, as were Keith Michell and Susan Hampshire at the Theatre Royal, Haymarket in London. That original production, with its thrilling story, its startling twists and its spectacular special effects, gave us an idea of the excitement that a Victorian audience must have experienced when watching a top-class melodrama. There have been many productions since, most notably in Los Angeles in 1981, when Charlton Heston played Sherlock Holmes, with Jeremy Brett as Dr Watson. Ten years later Heston took the part again, in a television film directed by his son Fraser.

The Incredible Murder of Cardinal Tosca by Alden Nowlan and Walter Learning is equally impressive, with an exciting, intelligent story of murder, black magic and international intrigue. In the original 1978 production at Fredericton, New Brunswick, Jack Medley as Holmes, Dan MacDonald as Watson and especially Vernon Chapman as Moriarty stood out in a very good cast. There have been subsequent productions in Canada and the United States, but for some reason the play has not achieved the popularity of *The Crucifer of Blood*, and it hasn't yet crossed the Atlantic.

The first really noteworthy minimalist play was written by Martyn Read as a solo piece for Nigel Stock, who had, in the 1960s, been the definitive Dr Watson on British television. In *221B* Watson made a sad and, he believed, final visit to Baker Street, following the death of his friend at the Reichenbach Falls. The furniture and objects in Holmes's sitting room inspired recollections of their adventures together, which in turn provoked comments on the detective's virtues and his shortcomings. Alone on stage, Stock presented a whole cast of characters, all recreated from the memories of Dr Watson. It was a masterly performance.

In 1985, having played Holmes on television with some success, Tom Baker took the part again in *The Mask of Moriarty* at the Gate Theatre in Dublin. Hugh Leonard's complex but carefully organised plot involves satire, slapstick, characters from Stevenson and Hornung, cross-dressing and plastic surgery. Professor Moriarty has survived Reichenbach, and now wears the face of Sherlock Holmes. Geoffrey Palmer played the dual role at the Leicester Haymarket in 1987, and the play has since been produced in America.

The year 1988 brought three major productions. Like Jerome Coopersmith, Leslie Bricusse was inspired by the work of Lerner and Loewe when he wrote the book, lyrics and music for *Sherlock Holmes: The Musical*. The original production – with Ron Moody and Liz Robertson, both highly successful in the genre, as Sherlock Holmes and Bella Moriarty – did well in Exeter before transferring to the West End, but there, luck was against it. A transport strike helped keep audiences away, and the show closed early. There was a national tour in 1993, with Robert Powell as Holmes, and since then the play, retitled *The Revenge of Sherlock Holmes*, has become very popular with amateur operatic societies.

Holmes and the Ripper by Brian Clemens was a much darker affair, based on the same outlandish conspiracy theory that inspired the film *Murder by Decree*. Francis Matthews and Frank Windsor were well cast as Holmes and Watson, confronting misguided monarchists, totalitarian Freemasons, and an insane surgeon. Since the original touring production, the play has been staged by both professional and amateur companies.

The Secret of Sherlock Holmes, at Wyndham's Theatre and then on tour, gave audiences the chance to see the now famous partnership of Jeremy Brett and Edward Hardwicke live on stage. Unlike *221B*, Jeremy Paul's play was a two-hander: just Holmes and Watson, vividly brought to life. The detective's 'secret' was revealed in the second act. He was Professor Moriarty. (Or was he? Some elements of the play suggest otherwise.) The actors and the production generally were widely praised, though there were some doubts about the play itself. Even so, there was another successful run in the West End in 2010, with Peter Egan and Robert Daws.

In 1998 the outstanding duo called Lip Service (otherwise known as Maggie Fox and Sue Ryding), who specialise in literary parodies, added the Great Detective to their repertoire. In *Move Over Moriarty*, investigation of the Garibaldi Biscuit Murders involves Holmes and Watson with such eccentric music-hall acts as Elsie Linnett, the Generously Proportioned Bulgarian Songthrush, and Death-Defying Dan and his Whelk-Infested Tank of Terror. Maggie Fox and Sue Ryding play all the characters, and the result is deliciously crazy comedy.

Sherlock Holmes – The Last Act! has not yet made it to the West End, but Roger Llewellyn has taken the play – written for him by David Stuart Davies – all over the world since 1999. Holmes has just returned from his friend's funeral, and, as we gradually realise, he is dying. The premise is similar to that of *221B*, but this is more profound, revealing great depths to the detective's character. In 2008 Llewellyn began touring with a quite different one-man play, also written by David Stuart Davies. *Sherlock Holmes – The Death and Life* is a fantastic comedy. Arthur Conan Doyle created Professor Moriarty to destroy Sherlock Holmes, but Moriarty rebels and Holmes refuses to die. As before, Roger Llewellyn's superb acting does justice to an excellent script.

The Hound of the Baskervilles remains the dramatists's favourite. In 2007 and 2008 Peter Egan and Philip Franks toured with a striking production, dramatised by Clive Francis. At the same time, the theatre company Illyria was performing a different adaptation in open-air venues around the UK. But the biggest success was the brilliant parody written by John Nicholson

Roger Llewellyn in
*Sherlock Holmes – The
Last Act! Courtesy of Roger
Llewellyn*

and Steve Canny and performed by the trio called Peepolykus. Nicholson was a bewildered Watson, Jason Thorpe a charming, rather dim-witted Sir Henry Baskerville, and Javier Marzan... Well, Marzan is Spanish and has a distinctive accent. So he played Holmes – and Mr and Mrs Barrymore, Mr and Miss Stapleton, and several other characters. It was completely mad and wonderfully funny, fully deserving the run at the Duchess Theatre that followed the national tour. There have since been successful productions in the United States.

There is one remarkably successful recent American play that has yet to cross the ocean. *Sherlock Holmes: The Final Adventure* by Steven Dietz is an acknowledged adaptation of

Sherlock Holmes by Arthur Conan Doyle and William Gillette. Dietz's version, first performed at Tucson, Arizona, in 2006, replaces Alice Faulkner with Irene Adler, introduces the King of Bohemia, and concludes just after the fight at the Reichenbach Falls. In 2007 it won the Mystery Writers of America's Edgar Allan Poe Award for best play, and it sometimes seems that every month, somewhere in the United States, there's a new professional production of *Sherlock Holmes: The Final Adventure*.

6

'DRAMATIC ENTRANCES AND EXITS'

• HOLMES ON THE BIG SCREEN •

SHERLOCK HOLMES MADE HIS moving picture debut in 1900, only a few years after the first successful demonstration of Edison's Kinetoscope. *Sherlock Holmes Baffled* was made by the American Mutoscope and Biograph Company for viewing in those machines that you used to find on seaside piers, where you looked through a slot and turned a handle to flick the pictures on and give the illusion of movement. It lasts about a minute and shows a burglar entering Holmes's apartment and robbing it before the detective's astonished eyes, vanishing by means of primitive stop-motion trick photography every time Holmes goes to seize him, and finally disappearing altogether. That's all! *Sherlock Holmes Baffled* is accessible anywhere now on YouTube or at www.archive.org/details/SherlockHolmesBaffled.

Other films, all silent, lasting no more than 20 minutes and nearly all long since lost, followed in pretty short order.

In 1905, Maurice Costello, the first named actor to play Holmes, appeared in the American *Sherlock Holmes; or, Held for Ransom*. Most of these early films were made in Europe – in Denmark, France, Italy and Germany – and the detective faced such popular villains as A.J. Raffles and Arsène Lupin. It was left to the English and the French to present something like the authentic Sherlock Holmes. Georges Treville, who also played Holmes, directed eight films during 1912 and 1913, all based on Conan Doyle's original stories. Advertisements claimed that the author himself was involved in the productions.

The first actor to be instantly recognisable as Sherlock Holmes was not an actor at all. James Bragington – gaunt, aquiline, and hawk-eyed – worked in the office of the British producer G.B. Samuelson and was spotted there by the director of *A Study in Scarlet*. The film is lost, but it does seem to have been remarkably faithful to its source. A couple of years later, Samuelson produced another close adaptation, *The Valley of Fear*, with H.A. Saintsbury as Holmes, a part he had played many times on stage, both in Conan Doyle's play *The Speckled Band* and in William Gillette's *Sherlock Holmes*.

This brings us to Gillette himself. He finally committed his own performance as Holmes to film in 1916, seventeen years after he had first played the part on stage. One reviewer remarked: 'William Gillette as Sherlock Holmes, in moving pictures, even at the ripe age of sixty-three years, was a consummation devoutly to be wished.' Alas, Gillette's *Sherlock Holmes* is yet another lost film. In England, meanwhile, a rival emerged, and most of his pictures do survive.

From 1921 to 1923 Eille Norwood played Sherlock Holmes in an astonishing total of forty-five short and two feature-length films for the Stoll Picture Company. He was much of an age with William Gillette, and, just as Gillette *was* Sherlock Holmes to a generation of theatregoers, so, in Britain at least, Norwood was to a generation of viewers. In *Memories and Adventures* Conan Doyle said: 'He has that rare quality which can only be described as glamour, which compels you to watch an actor eagerly even when he is doing nothing. He has a brooding eye which excites expectation, and he has a quite unrivalled power of disguise.' Hubert Willis, his Watson, was the first of note in the movies, though he was quite as old as Norwood, and appeared white-haired and clean-shaven throughout. (In *The Sign of Four* he was replaced by a younger actor, Arthur Cullin, so that Watson shouldn't appear too old to woo the heroine, Mary Morstan.)

The last notable silent film was made in 1922 by a major Hollywood studio, Goldwyn Pictures, but it was shot in England, with extensive location work. *Sherlock Holmes* (retitled *Moriarty* in Britain) was based on William Gillette's play, and set at the beginning of the detective's career. Holmes was played by a younger and much better-known actor than Eille Norwood: John Barrymore. His Watson was Roland Young in his first major part, and Barrymore later remarked: 'that quiet agreeable bastard had stolen every damned scene.'

The first talkie starred 'Hollywood's Perfect Englishman', Clive Brook, as Holmes. Though rather oddly entitled *The Return of Sherlock Holmes*, it bears little relationship to the book of the same name. The action occurs mostly on an ocean liner, and of course Professor Moriarty is involved. Brook played the detective again four years later. The new film was called *Sherlock Holmes*, and it brought Holmes up to date with a vengeance, to the extent of inventing a ludicrous superscientific device for stopping a criminal's getaway car by projecting an invisible ray.

In the 1931 British film *The Speckled Band*, Holmes, played by Raymond Massey in his first screen role, has an office with secretaries, filing cabinets, typewriters, and even a primitive computer. But, once those are out of the way, we are plunged into an atmospheric version of one of the best of the short stories. Massey, always a fine actor, is matched with one of the best villains going, Lyn Harding, who had played Dr Grimesby Rylott (*sic*) many times on stage; the part was well suited to his rather old-fashioned, barnstorming style.

As in the silent era there were many short parodies. *Lost in Limehouse, or Lady Esmeralda's Predicament*, one of a series of spoof melodramas made by the Masquers Club of Hollywood in 1933, is as fresh, anarchic and downright funny now as when it was made. Sheerluck Jones, called in when the beautiful daughter of the Duke of Dunkwell is abducted by a moustache-twirling villain (John Sheehan), is played by Olaf Hytten, who would later take various more sober roles in support of Basil Rathbone's Sherlock Holmes.

Two more feature films from the early 1930s deserve notice. In a British version of *The Hound of the Baskervilles*, Robert Rendel is a very acceptable Holmes, matched by the sturdy, sensible Watson of Fred Lloyd, though Edgar Wallace's dialogue is rather tiresomely jokey. The plot of *A Study in*

Scarlet, made by a small American company, is actually a clever variant on the theme of *And Then There Were None*, though it predates Agatha Christie's novel by several years. Reginald Owen, stocky, with a square, humorous face, isn't ideally cast as Sherlock Holmes, but the film is well made and jolly.

Few would call Rendel's and Owen's performances definitive, but Arthur Wontner, tall, thin and hawk faced, was like a *Strand* illustration come to life. His was a Holmes of retirement age, a gentlemanly and rather avuncular Holmes, but entirely authoritative. Wontner's five films were much closer to the real thing than any since Eille Norwood's time, and one at least was a classic. *The Triumph of Sherlock Holmes* is based on *The Valley of Fear*, though the writers, with some justification, have added Professor Moriarty as an active character.

It is worth noting here that all Holmes movies up until 1939 were given a contemporary setting. To cinema audiences, at least, the detective was a modern figure. Today's filmmakers give the same treatment to James Bond, whose true period is the Cold War of the 1950s and '60s.

The change came with *The Hound of the Baskervilles*, for which London and Dartmoor of the 1890s were recreated in Hollywood. The star, though he was originally billed below the romantic leads, was Basil Rathbone, still regarded by many as the perfect Sherlock Holmes. It's a superb film, with a superb Holmes at its heart: entirely convincing as thinker, dreamer and man of action. Nigel Bruce's Watson was the first to make a real impression, and is still rightly remembered with great affection, but it is hard to imagine this old duffer writing those magnificent accounts for *The Strand Magazine*.

The familiar faces of Nigel Bruce and Basil Rathbone, stars of fourteen Sherlock Holmes films and countless radio plays. *Collection of Roger Johnson and Jean Upton*

The partnership continued in *The Adventures of Sherlock Holmes*: cunning, suspenseful, atmospheric and, above all, tremendous fun, particularly in the delicious verbal sparring between Holmes and George Zucco's excellent Moriarty.

When America entered the war Rathbone and Bruce moved to a different studio. Holmes and Watson had played their part against the Kaiser, and it must have seemed only right that they should be seen in action against the Führer. *Sherlock Holmes and the Voice of Terror*, based in part on 'His Last Bow' and inspired by the derisive broadcasts of Lord Haw-Haw, was the first of five films with a contemporary wartime theme. They were followed by seven more, still set in the present day, but without the wartime references. All are well crafted, and the best of them – *The Spider Woman*, *The Scarlet Claw* and *The Pearl of Death* – are very good, though by now Watson, played by Nigel Bruce, seems a quite different person from the one that Conan Doyle created.

———⚬⊙⊙⚬———

Colour enters the picture as late as 1959, in *The Hound of the Baskervilles*, made in England by Hammer Films. Andre Morell was an excellent Watson, stalwart, loyal, and intelligent, and Peter Cushing, who was a Holmes devotee, gave a meticulous and careful performance as the detective. It's a handsome and undeniably exciting production, but very uneven, partly because the scriptwriter took too many liberties with the plot, and partly because Holmes is made to look small. Leading roles are played by two of the tallest men in British film, Christopher Lee and Francis De Wolff, who tower above the 5ft 10in Cushing.

Perhaps Christopher Lee should have been cast as Holmes? In 1962 he was, in a German / Italian / French black-and-white co-production called *Sherlock Holmes and the Deadly Necklace*.

Unfortunately every performance, including Lee's, was dubbed by American actors, and the incongruous result, with an equally unsympathetic jazz score, a tortuous script and humdrum direction, makes for a deeply flawed but perversely entertaining film.

Fortunately, in 1965 *A Study in Terror* gave us an admirable Holmes and Watson in John Neville and Donald Houston in a clever and highly atmospheric original story, pitting the Great Detective and the doctor against the great monster, Jack the Ripper. Among a fine cast, Robert Morley and Frank Finlay stand out as Mycroft Holmes and Inspector Lestrade.

Billy Wilder's 1970 film *The Private Life of Sherlock Holmes* was not a commercial success, but it is bizarre, outrageous, inventive, funny – and ultimately charming. Aided by Colin Blakely as Watson, Robert Stephens's performance hints at great depths to the detective's character. Christopher Lee, cast against type, is a splendid Mycroft, but again the whole cast is exceptionally good. Miklos Rozsa's music, based on his own violin concerto, is outstanding, and the witty script makes *The Private Life of Sherlock Holmes* the most quotable of all the apocryphal adventures.

They Might Be Giants (1971) is not really about Holmes at all, but about a twentieth-century American who believes that he is Holmes. On one level the film is an examination of character and its place in society; on another, as you might expect from James Goldman, who wrote *The Lion in Winter*, it's a very clever and engaging comedy. George C. Scott and Joanne Woodward are quite excellent as the madman and his reluctant psychiatrist – whose name, of course, is Dr Watson.

The hero of *The Adventure of Sherlock Holmes's Smarter Brother* is not Mycroft Holmes but a hitherto unknown insanely jealous younger sibling named Sigerson. Sherlock and Watson (Douglas Wilmer and Thorley Walters) are played pretty straight, but Sigerson (Gene Wilder), his friend Orville Sacker (Marty Feldman), Professor Moriarty (Leo McKern) and the rest of the crew are well over the top. As a Sherlock Holmes film, it is a non-starter, but its energy and sheer youthful verve make it a highly entertaining comedy.

In *The Seven-Per-Cent Solution*, written by Nicholas Meyer and based on his best-selling novel, Holmes's cocaine addiction has progressed so far that Watson has to lure him to Vienna for treatment with the radical new techniques of Dr Sigmund Freud. Nicol Williamson really doesn't look like Holmes, but his nervous mannerisms, his rapid deductions, and his impatience with lesser minds are all part of an excellently observed performance. Robert Duvall as Watson is let down only by his unsuccessful attempt at an English accent. Alan Arkin is splendid as the young Freud. All in all, it's a handsome and very entertaining film.

Unfortunately the same can't be said of Peter Cook and Dudley Moore's contemptible 1977 send-up of *The Hound of the Baskervilles*, which wastes a very talented cast and ruins a few good jokes.

Murder By Decree, a compelling and highly atmospheric film, is, unlike *A Study in Terror*, based on a serious (if now discredited) theory about the identity of Jack the Ripper. Christopher Plummer gives an unexpectedly mellow performance as Holmes, and his relationship with the excellent

Watson of James Mason is a joy. It's a particular pleasure to welcome back Frank Finlay as Inspector Lestrade.

Young Sherlock Holmes (1985), otherwise *Young Sherlock Holmes and the Pyramid of Fear*, begins with Holmes and Watson meeting as schoolboys. We know they didn't, of course, but this is an admitted fantasy, providing great fun as it plays 'let's pretend'. Nicholas Rowe and Alan Cox could hardly be bettered as the young Holmes and Watson.

Basil Rathbone's voice is heard briefly in the Disney cartoon feature *Basil The Great Mouse Detective*, but, of course, the main character is actually Basil of Baker Street, who lives in the cellar of 221B, and is a detective as celebrated among mice as Holmes is among human beings. The characters are subtler and the action gentler in the original novels by Eve Titus, but the film, which marked a long-overdue return to the great and grand style of Disney animation, is great fun. Barrie Ingham's brilliant, slightly manic Basil is never overshadowed by the master criminal, Professor Ratigan, played with fiendish relish by Vincent Price.

What if Dr Watson were the real Baker Street detective? That's the premise of 1988's *Without a Clue* – a single joke that never feels overstretched. Watson (Ben Kingsley) has created the character of Sherlock Holmes as a front for his own genius, and has employed an actor, Reginald Kincaid, to impersonate Holmes for the police and public. Unfortunately, Kincaid (Michael Caine) is a drunken, womanising, cowardly second-rater. The script is witty, the performances sometimes dazzlingly funny.

O Xangô de Baker Street, a Brazilian-Portuguese co-production based on the novel by Jô Soares, is a sumptuous, intelligent film that deserves to be better known by English-speaking audiences. At the suggestion of Sarah Bernhardt, Dom Pedro, the Brazilian Emperor, summons Holmes (Joaquim de Almeida) and Watson (Anthony Dawson) to Rio de Janeiro to investigate the theft of his Stradivarius violin. The dialogue is variously in English, French and Portuguese, with subtitles.

Guy Ritchie's *Sherlock Holmes* was released amid worldwide publicity in 2009, to immediate commercial success. Holmes, played by Robert Downey Jr, falls well short of the 'catlike love of personal cleanliness' that Watson remarks on, and he isn't 'rather over six feet, and so excessively lean that he [seems] to be considerably taller', but he's a compelling actor, and he's well matched by Jude Law's Watson. Their relationship, with its ups and downs, is thoroughly believable. The story is fantastic – you could drive a train through some of the holes in the plot – but it moves along at a cracking pace, and thanks to some amazing CGI work it all looks superb.

The even more spectacular 2011 sequel *Sherlock Holmes: A Game of Shadows* introduces Professor Moriarty, played with urbane menace by Jared Harris. Having anonymously taken over the great armaments factories of Europe, he aims to profit by provoking revolution and war. Ranged against him are Holmes, Watson and their unexpected Gypsy ally: the lithe and deadly Madame Simza. Watching anxiously in London are Mycroft Holmes (Stephen Fry) and Mary Watson. The plot this time is coherent as well as epic. There's action aplenty, and, as in the first film, you can actually see Holmes thinking.

For the first time in more than sixty years Sherlock Holmes has proved popular enough with cinema-goers to justify a series of films. As we write, the third is being prepared. Holmes himself would no doubt say: 'The old wheel turns, and the same spoke comes up. It's all been done before, and will be again.'

7

'A WELL-KNOWN VOICE'

· HOLMES ON RADIO AND AUDIO ·

IT WAS AN AMERICAN who launched Sherlock Holmes and Dr Watson onto the airwaves. In 1930, shortly after the death of Sir Arthur Conan Doyle, an actress and writer named Edith Meiser decided that radio lacked drama, that Sherlock Holmes was the ideal hero, and that William Gillette was the right person to portray him. Gillette was 77 and still touring; he wouldn't be tied to a radio contract, but his performance in Miss Meiser's adaptation of *The Adventure of the Speckled Band* for NBC, with Leigh Lovell as Dr Watson, ensured the success of the series that followed, in which Richard Gordon (and, for a year, Louis Hector) played the detective. All too soon, Edith Meiser began to run short of suitable stories, but her contract allowed her to devise new ones. From January 1933, Meiser's stories outnumbered Conan Doyle's.

In November 1935 William Gillette returned, in a 60-minute version of his famous play *Sherlock Holmes*, adapted for Lux Radio Theater by Edith Meiser. Neither of Gillette's radio performances has survived. However, his voice can still be heard in a couple of scenes from his play, recorded in 1936 at the house of a Harvard academic who read Watson's lines while his wife played Alice Faulkner. Even in his 80s, Gillette was the authentic Holmes.

The play was adapted again in 1938, this time by Orson Welles for *The Mercury Theatre on the Air*. In *The Immortal Sherlock Holmes*, Welles actually impersonated Gillette's performance. Introducing the drama, he said: 'It is too little to say that William Gillette resembled Sherlock Holmes. Sherlock Holmes looks exactly like William Gillette. Sounds like him too, we're afraid...'

Holmes and Watson finally arrived on British radio that same year, in *Sherlock Holmes and the Adventure of Silver Blaze*, with a cast headed by F. Wyndham Goldie. Meanwhile, in America, Basil Rathbone and Nigel Bruce made such an impression in the 1939 film *The Hound of the Baskervilles* that they were quickly signed up by NBC and just as quickly proved that they were entirely at home on the air, with scripts written, as before, by Edith Meiser. British listeners made do with the occasional single play, such as *The Boscombe Valley Mystery*, broadcast on the BBC Home Service in 1943, in which, we're told, Arthur Wontner gave his customary calm, authoritative performance as Holmes. His Watson was Carleton Hobbs.

In 1944 Leslie Charteris and Denis Green took over as writers for the American series, bringing a freshness and a new authenticity to the scripts. When Charteris left to concentrate upon his own character, The Saint, he was succeeded by Anthony Boucher, who, in partnership with Green, created

an astonishing number of dazzlingly clever, literate and satis-
fyingly dramas, in which Rathbone's Holmes was less brusque
and Bruce's Watson less scatterbrained than in their films. In
1945 Sir Cedric Hardwicke and Finlay Currie played Holmes
and Watson for the BBC, in John Dickson Carr's full-blooded
adaptation of *The Speckled Band*, a production that was heard
again recently on BBC Radio 4 Extra. No recording exists
of the other production that year: *Silver Blaze*, with Laidman
Browne and Norman Shelley.

In 1946 Basil Rathbone declined to play Holmes again.
Nigel Bruce continued to play Watson on radio with Tom
Conway as Holmes, but both left after a year and were
replaced by John Stanley and Alfred Shirley. The series sol-
diered on, with scripts by Edith Meiser and others; it finally
petered out in 1950. Ben Wright and Eric Snowden were the
last Holmes and Watson. Then, after a brief hiatus, the ini-
tiative passed to Britain, when Carleton Hobbs and Norman
Shelley embarked on a partnership that would last for seventeen years.

From 1952 to 1957, Hobbs and Shelley's performances
were nearly all in dramatisations by Felix Felton, broadcast
as part of BBC Radio's *Children's Hour*. No recordings are
known to exist, and the same is true, sadly, of the one exception. In 1953 Raymond Raikes adapted William Gillette's
play as a 90-minute drama. Hobbs and Shelley, of course,
played Sherlock Holmes and Dr Watson, and that fine actor
Frederick Valk was Professor Moriarty.

In 1954, listeners could also hear a completely different
series on the BBC. This series was written by John Keir Cross,

and featured Sir John Gielgud and Sir Ralph Richardson as Holmes and Watson, with Orson Welles as Moriarty in 'The Final Problem'. (Gielgud's famously beautiful voice was very unlike the 'high, strident' tones that Watson ascribes to Holmes in his accounts, but would listeners ever accept a Holmes who did sound like that? Some later actors with mellifluous voices have also enjoyed success in the role: most notably Clive Merrison and Jeremy Brett.) Only twelve of the sixteen plays were broadcast here. American audiences got the lot shortly afterwards, but in the UK we had to wait until recordings were released on cassette and CD.

After their *Children's Hour* series, Hobbs and Shelley plunged into a grand six-part serial, *The Hound of the Baskervilles*, again written by Felix Felton. In 1959 they began a ten-year association with Michael Hardwick, whose four-dozen scripts were all authentic and nicely paced. (In 1967 the South African Broadcasting Corporation used twelve of them for a pleasant series.) Carleton Hobbs as Holmes may lack the manic quality and even rudeness of some recent interpretations, but there's a refreshingly astringent quality to his voice and he always convinces. Norman Shelley's Watson is superficially like Nigel Bruce's, with his brandy-and-cigars voice, but he's sensible and intelligent, as well as brave and compassionate. For British Holmesians who grew up in the 1950s and '60s, these were the true Holmes and Watson. (Felix Felton wasn't entirely sidelined. His five-part version of *The Sign of Four*, with Richard Hurndall as Holmes, was broadcast in 1959, and two years later he adapted *The Hound* again for Hobbs and Shelley, this time as a 90-minute play.)

Michael Hardwick reworked *A Study in Scarlet* in 1974 for Robert Powell and Dinsdale Landen, who actually sounded like the young fellows that Holmes and Watson were when they first met. Otherwise there was no more Holmesian drama until 1977, when the American company CBS included nine competent adaptations in its *Radio Mystery Theater* series, with Kevin McCarthy as Holmes. The following year, BBC Radio 4 transmitted thirteen good adaptations, with Barry Foster as a fine, incisive Holmes, with David Buck as a sturdy Watson.

In 1978 Canadian listeners heard Alden Nowlan and Walter Learning's thrilling melodrama *The Incredible Murder of Cardinal Tosca*. Most of the original stage cast were retained, but John Neville played Sherlock Holmes, having made his mark with the character on screen and stage. This production is almost unknown outside Canada, and seems to have been unjustly forgotten there.

From 1979 to 1985, South Africa's Springbok Radio featured Graham Armitage and Kerry Jordan in forty-eight intelligent and entertaining new adventures under the title *The Stories of Sherlock Holmes*. British radio first tackled pastiche in 1981: John Moffatt and Timothy West were excellent in Glyn Dearman's *Sherlock Holmes vs Dracula*, but David March almost stole the show as the vampire count, a part he had already played twice. Perhaps because of the rich atmosphere and the immediacy of the action, the play is actually more effective than Loren Estleman's original novel.

In 1983 came Grant Eustace's *Second Holmes*: six witty and inventive investigations by the grandsons of Sherlock and John. Stamford Holmes (Peter Egan) has inherited his forebear's genius but thinks that crime detection is a job for the police. He has to be goaded by his friend (Jeremy Nicholas), who is keen to uphold the tradition of their families.

The Mystery of the Reluctant Storyteller by Derek Wilson combined drama and metaphysical speculation, as Holmes and Watson, played by Mark Wing-Davey and Andrew Hilton, discussed their creator and his motives. Hilton returned as Dr Watson later in 1986, in a first-rate adaptation of *The Valley of Fear* by Roy Apps, who ingeniously rearranged the complex dual narrative for greater dramatic impact. Tim Pigott-Smith was an admirable Holmes.

In 1987 the centenary of the detective's first appearance in print was the spur for several radio documentaries, but the only drama was a series of half-hour plays by Grant Eustace, based on Conan Doyle's stories and featuring Roy Marsden and John Moffatt as Holmes and Watson. They were first heard as entertainment on transatlantic flights, and were then made available as audio cassettes. None were broadcast, in Britain at least, until 1993.

Cecil Jenkins's thought-provoking *The Singular Case of Sherlock H. and Sigmund F.* was, uniquely for a Sherlock Holmes play, transmitted on BBC Radio 3, the broadcaster's highbrow channel, in 1988. Ronald Pickup and Norman Rodway headed a distinguished cast. More important though, was *The Hound of the Baskervilles*, dramatised for BBC Radio 4 by Bert Coules in a way that respected the listeners's intelligence and stretched their perception of how an audio play could be presented. Its success led to the commissioning of a huge project: the adaptation for radio of all four novels and all fifty-six short stories. The casting of Roger Rees and Crawford Logan in *The Hound* had attracted some criticism, and when Coules's version of *A Study in Scarlet* was recorded in 1989 Clive Merrison and Michael Williams played Holmes and Watson, roles they continued to inhabit for nearly nine years, quickly becoming a partnership to rival Rathbone and Bruce, Hobbs and Shelley, or Brett and Hardwicke. It would be hard to exaggerate the importance, and the sheer quality, of the whole project.

The BBC also offered some good single plays. Dinsdale Landen as Holmes and John Moffatt as Watson overacted gleefully in Charles Marowitz's bitter comedy *Sherlock's Last Case*. *The Adventure of the Pimlico Poisoner* had Holmes (William Chubb) investigating the sadistic murders committed by Dr Neill Cream. Simon Callow and Ian Hogg were impressive in *The Seven-per-Cent Solution* by Denny Martin Flinn, which curiously was more faithful to Nicholas Meyer's novel than Meyer himself had been when he adapted it for the cinema. Simon Callow returned, with Nicky Henson as Watson, in John Taylor's 1993 series *The Unopened Casebook of Sherlock Holmes*, in which Holmes investigated apparently impossible situations and seemingly supernatural phenomena. It went out on BBC Radio 5, which was not a 24-hour news channel at the time.

Edward Petherbridge and David Peart were excellent in a series made by a British company for National Public Radio in America. The skilful adaptations by Tim Crook and Richard Shannon had limited exposure in the UK and have been unfairly neglected since, but as we write they are being released in a new format, as interactive radio apps.

After several seemingly barren years, the Americans came to the fore again when, in 1998, writer and director Jim French added the Great Detective to his syndicated weekly drama series *Imagination Theater*. *The Further Adventures of Sherlock Holmes* was, and still is, gloriously reminiscent of the great days of American radio. John Gilbert played Holmes, with Lawrence Albert as Watson, until Gilbert's retirement in 2000. His replacement, John Patrick Lowrie, brings a similar incisive authority to the character, and his relationship with Larry Albert's Watson is beautifully judged. Jim French has been joined by other writers, from both sides of the ocean, the most prolific and most important being Matthew J. Elliott, who, in 2005, started the parallel series of Conan Doyle adaptations called *The Classic Adventures of Sherlock Holmes*, for which he has so far dramatised just over half of the sixty stories.

In 2000 BBC Radio 4 gave us a good four-part adaptation of Laurie R. King's novel, *The Beekeeper's Apprentice*, with James Fox as Holmes and Monica Dolan as the young Mary Russell. The following year, by contrast, David Mairowitz's curious comedy *A Capital Case – Karl Marx Meets Sherlock Holmes* had Marx (David de Keyser) requesting Holmes (Robert Bathurst) to recover the manuscript of *Das Kapital*.

Plans for a series of new plays by Bert Coules were disrupted when Michael Williams died in 2001, and a new Watson had to be found for Clive Merrison's brilliant, arrogant Holmes. Andrew Sachs proved to be the ideal replacement, and the first season of *The Further Adventures of Sherlock Holmes* aired in 2002. The mysteries baffled, the solutions satisfied, and the explanations revealed unexpected depths to the lives and personalities of the people concerned – including Holmes and Watson. There were fifteen *Further Adventures* in all, the last being 'The Marlbourne Point Mystery' in 2010. *The Sunday Times* rightly called the series 'a triumphant continuation of one of Radio 4's great achievements'.

Decades had passed since William Gillette's melodrama *Sherlock Holmes* was adapted for audio, but two recordings emerged within two years in America. David Warner took the lead in Peggy Webber's production for California Artists Radio Theatre, and Martin Jarvis was Holmes for Yuri Rasovsky and the Hollywood Theatre of the Ear. The latter may be preferable, being unabridged (it was released with a complete recording of Conan Doyle's 1910 play *The Speckled Band*), but both are quality productions. A more radical adaptation was produced in 2010 for the Sherlock Holmes Society of London, as one of a series of audio plays performed by the Old Court Radio Theatre Company. Jim Crozier and Dave Hawkes, an excellent Holmes and Watson, are well matched by the magnificent Moriarty of Cyril Bagshaw. Since 2006 the company has recorded fifteen plays, mostly written by Matthew J. Elliott. All are freely accessible via the society's website at www.sherlock-holmes.org.uk/world/radio.php.

The latest big player in the game is production company Big Finish, which made its name with books and audio plays based on *Doctor Who*. In 2009 the company released recordings of *Sherlock Holmes – The Last Act!* and *Sherlock Holmes – The Death and Life*, the two one-man plays written by David Stuart

Davies for the actor Roger Llewellyn. Thanks to Llewellyn's superb performances, Davies's inspired scripts, and to the careful supervision of Nicholas Briggs, these are productions to treasure. Briggs, who had played Holmes on stage with style and authority, takes the lead in the rest of the Big Finish productions, with Richard Earl as his stalwart Watson. Beginning with Brian Clemens's sensational play *Holmes and the Ripper*, they alternate Conan Doyle's original stories with tales by other writers, in a series of richly atmospheric and exciting dramas that shows no sign of flagging.

Laurence Owen's 2011 production of *The Hound of the Baskervilles* (available for download at http://corporaterecords. co.uk) makes such strikingly imaginative use of music and sound effects to complement a fine cast that his description of it as a 'radio film' seems justified.

A WORD ABOUT AUDIOBOOKS

There are so many recorded readings of Sherlock Holmes stories that the best we can do is to point you towards some that we know are really good. The very best complete readings, we think, are those by David Timson for Naxos AudioBooks and those by Derek Jacobi for AudioGO. There are also outstanding recordings of selected stories by Basil Rathbone (Caedmon), Robert Hardy (Argo), Douglas Wilmer (Penguin, and Porter Press International), and Peter Cushing (Cosmic Hobo).

8

'ACTORS IN THIS DRAMA'

• HOLMES ON THE SMALL SCREEN •

SHERLOCK HOLMES FIRST APPEARED on television in America, played by Louis Hector – already known as Holmes to radio listeners – in a 1937 version of 'The Three Garridebs'. No recording exists, but the next production, from 1949, does survive. This was *The Speckled Band*, in which Holmes was played by Alan Napier, later to become famous as Alfred the butler to Adam West's Batman. It's a competent, often unintentionally comic adaptation, let down by Melville Cooper's depiction of Watson as a burbling idiot.

Holmes's first appearance on British television was in a live BBC production of *The Mazarin Stone*, part of a series called *For the Children*. Andrew Osborn played Holmes, but when six more plays were made later in 1951 he was replaced by Alan Wheatley, whose Watson was Raymond Francis. This series, the first ever made for television, was favourably reviewed, and stills show that it was handsomely designed. There were no recordings, though a rather less successful production from the same year was recorded: *The Man Who Disappeared*, based with some licence on 'The Man with the Twisted Lip', was made on film as the intended first of a series, but the uninspired performances of John Longden and Campbell Singer as Holmes and Watson are symptomatic of the production's generally tedious nature.

A far more notable achievement was a series of thirty-nine half-hour films made in France in 1954–55 by the American producer Sheldon Reynolds. Most of the stories are apocryphal, but on the whole pretty neat. Sets and costumes are good, and the largely British cast, led by Ronald Howard as a likeable, uncomplicated Holmes, Howard Marion Crawford as a solid, no-nonsense Watson, and Archie Duncan as an unexpectedly bulky, Scottish Inspector Lestrade, are more than adequate. Twenty-five years later, Reynolds went to Poland with Geoffrey Whitehead and Donald Pickering to make a second series, this time in colour. For uncertain reasons, however, it was never widely distributed and is usually considered inferior to its predecessor.

In 1964 Holmes returned to the BBC, in a version of 'The Speckled Band', included in a series called *Detective*, which led to the same leading actors joining forces again the following year for a series of twelve. Some of the stories suffered a little from being stretched to fill a 50-minute format, but the standard was high. Douglas Wilmer and Nigel Stock were hailed by many as the definitive Holmes and Watson of their generation, and there were particularly good performances from Peter Madden as Lestrade and Derek Francis as Mycroft in an excellent adaptation of 'The Bruce-Partington Plans'.

'An actor, and a rare one.' Douglas Wilmer (right) was Sherlock Holmes on television in the 1960s and on film in 1975. In 2012 he had a cameo role in 'The Reichenbach Fall' episode of BBC's *Sherlock*. Tim Pigott-Smith (left) played Dr Watson on stage and Sherlock Holmes on BBC radio. They met at the 2010 annual dinner of the Sherlock Holmes Society of London, at the House of Commons. *Photo copyright Roger Johnson*

(Six of the plays were remade in Germany in 1967, with Erich Schellow and Paul Edwin Roth in the leading roles.) All but two of the series still exist and have been released on DVD – but only in North America and France.

Wilmer turned down the series that followed in 1968, and Peter Cushing was engaged, again with Nigel Stock as Watson. Thanks mainly to severe budgetary restrictions, the sixteen episodes were widely variable in quality, but the best are very good indeed and, unusually for the time, they were all made in colour. The two-part production of *The Hound of the Baskervilles* is considered by some experts to be the best screen version of the novel. Fortunately it is one of the five surviving instalments, and is available on DVD.

In 1972 Universal remade *The Hound of the Baskervilles* as a television film; its most notable feature is the way in which it recycles the sets from the pre-war Frankenstein films, so that one half expects the Burgomeister of Coombe Tracey to urge the peasants to go with their flaming torches and hunt down the monstrous hound. Bernard Fox bumbles as Watson, and Stewart Granger is just plain wrong as Sherlock Holmes. Many would say the same of Roger Moore in a much better film, *Sherlock Holmes in New York* – an ingenious story of an impossible bullion robbery – made because the 1890s New York set from *Hello, Dolly!* was available. Moore is too conventionally handsome, but he seizes the part with both hands and makes the most of his exchanges with John Huston's outrageously Irish Professor Moriarty.

Christopher Plummer first appeared as Holmes in a 1977 British adaptation of 'Silver Blaze', with reliable old Thorley Walters as Watson. The result is a brisk and very competent production that doesn't seem rushed at 30 minutes.

Parodies abounded in the 1970s. John Cleese made a couple of rather surreal television films, *Elementary My Dear Watson* and *The Strange Case of the End of Civilisation as we Know it*, which were entertaining but contained a good deal more of John Cleese than of Sherlock Holmes. Larry Hagman played Sherman Holmes, a Los Angeles cop who believed himself to be his near-namesake, in *The Return of the World's Greatest Detective*. The premise is similar, but the television film, though amusing, has neither the depth nor the charm of *They Might Be Giants*.

Something much more interesting and important was going on in the Soviet Union, where in 1979 Lenfilms produced the first in a series of dramatisations under the over-all title Приключения Шерлока Холмса и Доктора Ватсона (*The Adventures of Sherlock Holmes and Doctor Watson*). Western audiences must learn to accept a winding thoroughfare in Riga as Baker Street and a *dacha* in the steppes as Baskerville Hall, but the quality of the design, the direction and the acting makes acceptance surprisingly easy. Profound knowledge and love of the source material shine in every frame, not least in the performances of Vasily Livanov and Vitaly Solomin as Holmes and Watson. English-speaking viewers had to wait five years to enjoy such authentic depictions of the detective and the doctor.

In 1982, the BBC adapted *The Hound of the Baskervilles* as a faithful and good-looking four-part serial, with Holmes played by Tom Baker. It was a bold choice, as by then he was indelibly identified with *Doctor Who*, but in fact he gives a very good performance. His Watson, Terence Rigby, is brave and loyal, every inch the one-time rugger player, but he's also rather too stolid and given to mumbling like Nigel Bruce. This is a pity, because on the whole the production is very agreeable. In the same year Granada Television made an original drama serial: *Young Sherlock: The Mystery of the Manor House*. Guy Henry is excellent as the 16-year-old Holmes, who returns from boarding school to find his family gone and their house occupied by aristocratic bullies. It looks good, and the writer, Gerald Frow, clearly knows his Conan Doyle, but it is too long at 4½ hours, and the story rather peters out at the end. The BBC did rather better with a crisp, clever and charming series called *The Baker Street Boys*. Holmes and Watson are glimpsed occasionally, but the detective's little band of street urchins, the Baker Street Irregulars, are definitely the main characters, applying the methods that he taught them.

In 1983 Peter O'Toole lent his voice to four annoyingly incompetent Australian cartoon films, based on the four long stories. The backgrounds are sometimes beautiful, but the characters are crudely drawn, the animation is basic, the scripts poor, and O'Toole seems to be talking in his sleep.

It was time for something classy, but the two films made that year by Mapleton Films didn't quite make it. Ian Richardson is a fine Holmes in *The Sign of Four*, and there are good turns from the rest of the cast, but David Healy, though likeable as Watson, makes little impression. The film is entertaining, but the story has been unnecessarily and unsuccessfully sensationalised. As he was unavailable for *The Hound of the Baskervilles*, Healy's place was taken by Donald Churchill, who gave a similarly unmemorable performance. Ian Richardson deserved something better, and in time he got it when he was cast as Dr Joseph Bell in a fictional series about the man who inspired Arthur Conan Doyle to create Sherlock Holmes. (A planned third Sherlock Holmes – *Hands of a Murderer* – eventually emerged in 1990, with Edward Woodward seriously miscast in the lead. It is remarkably poor.)

The excellence that we'd longed for was provided by Granada, in a magnificent and accurate series based firmly on Conan Doyle's original stories, which reached our screens in 1984. David Burke is the authentic Dr Watson: impetuous, intelligent, humorous, loyal, courageous and sufficiently tolerant to bear with the moody eccentricities of Jeremy Brett's

Holmes. Brett gives us the true manic depressive that we see in the pages of *The Strand Magazine*, the man who loathes every form of society with the whole of his Bohemian soul: the genius and the loner. The first set was a winner all round, and the second lived up to it, culminating as it did in a superb adaptation of 'The Final Problem'. Eric Porter oscillates wonderfully in an electrifyingly sinister performance as Professor Moriarty, and location filming was never better used than in the fatal conflict at the Reichenbach Falls.

When Burke, at his own suggestion, was replaced by Edward Hardwicke, the series maintained its superior quality. The feature-length film of *The Sign of Four* may well be the best-ever screen version of any of the four long stories. After that the level was less consistent; *The Hound of the Baskervilles* was disappointingly anaemic, partly because of Brett's medical problems and partly because of changes in the television industry. By 1994, when the last of the episodes was broadcast, there had been half a dozen truly unfortunate films in the series, their inferiority made more obvious by contrast with the two dozen or so of the best, which are superb.

There was a Christmas treat in 1984. A fine story and script had tempted Peter Cushing to take up the deerstalker again and portray the elderly Holmes foiling a devilish plot that prefigures the First World War. In *The Masks of Death*, everything is right: script, direction, design, casting and, among a distinguished cast, the performances of Cushing and John Mills as Sherlock Holmes and Dr Watson stand out. Their companionable relationship is pure delight, and they are well supported by a cast that includes Gordon Jackson, who is Inspector MacDonald to the life.

In *The Return of Sherlock Holmes* Michael Pennington's Holmes is revived from cryogenic sleep by Jane Watson (Margaret Colin), the American great-granddaughter of his old friend, and the two are soon deep in a clever murder mystery. The idea of the Great Detective, with his Victorian knowledge and preconceptions, finding his way in a new world, would be used again, first in *1994 Baker Street: Sherlock Holmes Returns*, which certainly has its good points, including Anthony Higgins, and more successfully in an animated series called *Sherlock Holmes in the 22nd Century*. But *The Return of Sherlock Holmes* has a charm and a wit that the later films seem to lack.

In 1991 Christopher Lee and Patrick Macnee had a go at the retirement-age Holmes and Watson in two entertaining but over-long films that took the pair to foreign parts. *Sherlock Holmes and the Leading Lady* involves them with Irene Adler once again and a plot against the Austrian Emperor, while in *Incident at Victoria Falls* they are commissioned by King Edward to take an enormously valuable diamond to South Africa. The location work gives the second film a very attractive and spectacular quality, and Lee in particular is on good form in both.

Fraser Heston scripted and directed *The Crucifer of Blood*, a decent but not outstanding film version of Paul Giovanni's play, starring Charlton Heston, who had played Holmes in a Los Angeles production a decade earlier, with Jeremy Brett as Dr Watson. This time Richard Johnson was the good doctor, and though the two men were rather too old for the parts, they worked nicely together.

Few would have thought of Matt Frewer as obvious casting for Sherlock Holmes. Nevertheless, he played the part in four feature-length Canadian films, beginning in 2000 with an adequate version of *The Hound of the Baskervilles* and ending with an exciting but entirely apocryphal piece called *The Case of the Whitechapel Vampire*. Frewer's mannerisms can become irritating, but Holmes is given a firm anchor by the intelligent and steadfast Watson of Kenneth Welsh.

The Canadian *Hound* is far from perfect, but it's no worse than the BBC's production of 2002. Richard E. Grant, who would be an excellent Holmes, is cast as Stapleton, while Richard Roxburgh, who would make a good Watson, is Holmes, and Watson is played by Ian Hart, who would be rather good as Lestrade... Holmes gratuitously beats up a cabby to get information from him, and injects himself with cocaine while on the case, and the Holmes and Watson relationship is of mutual mistrust. It's all wrong! The computer-generated hound is sadly unimpressive. The same team returned with an original and rather distasteful story called *Sherlock Holmes and the Case of the Silk Stocking* but with a new Holmes in Rupert Everett, who does at least seem intellectual, though his perpetual moody frown gets tiresome. Also the very noticeable fact that he's 8in taller than Ian Hart is distracting.

Sherlock: Case of Evil is something of a guilty pleasure. Like *Young Sherlock Holmes* it completely rewrites the origin of the Baker Street partnership, but in a much more contentious way. James D'Arcy is good as the arrogant, sexy young detective (yes, sexy), as is Roger Morlidge as the young pathologist and inventor, John H. Watson. Vincent D'Onofrio, looking like Bill Sikes, hams it up something lovely as Professor Moriarty. It's a long way from Conan Doyle but curiously entertaining.

Sherlock Holmes and the Baker Street Irregulars is less controversial, though there are some distracting anachronisms. Holmes (the excellent Jonathan Pryce) is framed for murder by master criminal Irene Adler, and Watson (the likewise excellent Bill Paterson) must save him, with the help of the Irregulars. It's very good in parts but lacks something in comparison with *The Baker Street Boys*.

Many thought that nothing now could rival the very best of the Granada series, and no Holmes could match the impression made by Jeremy Brett. They were proved wrong in 2010 when the first series of the BBC's *Sherlock* was broadcast. The detective has been brought into the present day before, but never with such skill and such utter conviction. *Sherlock* does the job thoroughly, remaking Holmes, Watson,

Benedict Cumberbatch on location in North Gower Street for 'The Reichenbach Fall', July 2011. *Photo copyright Jean Upton*

Lestrade, Mrs Hudson and the rest as people of the twenty-first century. Others have presented Holmes and Watson as the young men they really were, but always – at least since the John Barrymore *Sherlock Holmes* of 1922 – in stories that owed very little to Conan Doyle. But Steven Moffat and Mark Gatiss, the creators of *Sherlock*, are not only outstanding writers but Holmes devotees as well, and they've given us Benedict Cumberbatch and Martin Freeman in stories that are entirely of our time, though their roots are firmly in Conan Doyle. Cumberbatch and Freeman could hardly be improved upon as Sherlock and John. The critic Tom Sutcliffe remarked: 'Flagrantly unfaithful to the original in some respects, Sherlock is wonderfully loyal to it in every way that matters.'

Martin Freeman looking pensive at the doorway of 221B, July 2011. *Photo copyright Jean Upton*

The conclusion of the second series, with Watson sadly unaware that Holmes has survived an apparently fatal fall, engineered by Andrew Scott's insanely vicious Jim Moriarty, triggered an astonishingly widespread debate as to just how it was achieved. Whatever the explanation, it will almost certainly be a surprise.

As we write, CBS is planning a series called *Elementary*, which will place Sherlock Holmes, played by Jonny Lee Miller, in twenty-first-century New York. Rather more exciting is the news that filming began in late 2011 on a new Russian series, starring 34-year-old Igor Petrenko as Holmes and Andrey Panin as Watson.

9

'CONFOUND THAT WHINING MUSIC; IT GETS ON MY NERVES!'

• SHERLOCK HOLMES AND MUSIC •

HOLMES WAS, AS DR Watson noted, an enthusiastic musician. We find him attending recitals by two outstanding violinists of the time, Pablo Sarasate and Wilma Norman-Neruda, as well as a concert at the Albert Hall by an as-yet-unidentified singer whom he called Carina, an unspecified Wagner opera at Covent Garden, and a performance of Meyerbeer's *Les Huguenots* featuring the de Reszke brothers, Jean and Édouard. Moreover, Watson tells us that Holmes wrote a monograph on 'the Polyphonic Motets of Lassus', which, when printed for private circulation, was said by experts to be the last word upon the subject. (An impressive feat, but feasible, as Michael Procter explains in his recent monograph *Melancholia in Music: The Posthumous Motets of Orlandus Lassus*.)

His own instrument was the violin, though, as Watson reports in *A Study in Scarlet*, he approached it in an unconventional way:

I see that I have alluded above to his powers upon the violin. These were very remarkable, but as eccentric as all his other accomplishments. That he could play pieces, and difficult pieces, I knew well, because at my request he has played me some of Mendelssohn's Lieder, and other favourites. When left to himself, however, he would seldom produce any music or attempt any recognized air. Leaning back in his armchair of an evening, he would close his eyes and scrape carelessly at the fiddle which was thrown across his knee. Sometimes the chords were sonorous and melancholy. Occasionally they were fantastic and cheerful. Clearly they reflected the thoughts which possessed him, but whether the music aided those thoughts, or whether the playing was simply the result of a whim or fancy, was more than I could determine. I might have rebelled against these exasperating solos had it not been that he usually terminated them by playing in quick succession a whole series of my favourite airs as a slight compensation for the trial upon my patience.

He claimed that his own violin was a Stradivarius, though thousands of violins were made in tribute to Antonio Stradivari, copying his model and bearing labels that read 'Stradivarius'. Holmes would have known, though Watson probably didn't, that the presence of such a label isn't a guarantee that the instrument is a genuine Strad.

———

There have been successful musical plays about Sherlock Holmes. Besides *Baker Street* and *Sherlock Holmes: The Musical*, there is, for instance, Teddy Hayes's raucously entertaining *The Baskerville Beast*. There was the ballet *The Great Detective*, and in 1981 the City of Birmingham Choir performed a specially commissioned oratorio by John Dankworth and Benny Green, *The Diamond and the Goose*, based on 'The Blue Carbuncle'.

Holmes is the subject of at least two songs written and performed on the music hall stage in the 1890s. The detective's death was reported in *The Strand Magazine* in December 1893, and within a few months H.C. Barry was wowing the audiences with 'The Ghost of Sherlock Holmes':

> My life was more than misery:
> Condemned to strut the earth,
> And be a spy at beck and call
> Of those who gave me birth.
> But, now that I'm a spectre, all
> Their misdeeds shall recoil —
> I'm going to haunt 'Strand Magazine',
> 'Tit-Bits' and Conan Doyle!

Charles Bignell's song *Sherlock Holmes, D.T.* simply made fun of Holmes's remarkable DeTective powers, but Claude Ralston, in the unimaginatively titled 'Sherlock Holmes', was more topical, and his conclusion differed from Barry's:

> You say it is a pity that this splendid man should die.
> I think the Swiss tale is a plant, I'll give my reason why.
> There's a lady in the question, so he's gone and done a 'guy',
> But he'll turn up again, will Sherlock Holmes.

We have no record of Ralston's song being performed in the halls. It was published in the third edition of *The Scottish Students' Songbook* in 1897, and could still be found in later editions.

Most of the Holmes-related music on record comes from film or television soundtracks, or from stage musicals. A search on Amazon or eBay is probably the best initial move and may guide you towards one of the more unusual compositions, such as the jazz saxophonist Alan Barnes's *Sherlock Holmes Suite*, Carey Blyton's similarly titled *Sherlock Holmes Suite* for brass quintet, and Miklos Ròzsa's *Violin Concerto*, which the composer later adapted as the theme music for Billy Wilder's film *The Private Life of Sherlock Holmes*.

10

'THE OLD ROOMS IN BAKER STREET'

· 221B OR NOT 221B? ·

FROM VERY EARLY ON, one of the most hotly contested topics has been the location of 221B Baker Street. At the time of Holmes and Watson's residence, that address simply did not exist.

Until 1921, Baker Street's numbering ran consecutively up the east side, with nos 1 to 43 from Portman Square to Paddington Street; down the west side it was numbered 44 to 85 from Crawford Street to Portman Square. The section from Paddington Street/Crawford Street to Marylebone Road was called York Place, and the section from Marylebone Road to Regent's Park was Upper Baker Street. Each was separately numbered.

In 1921 York Place became part of Baker Street, and the entire street was renumbered, this time with even numbers on the east side and odd numbers on the west, running from south to north.

In 1930 Upper Baker Street was added, so that the whole street now ran from Portman Square to Park Road, and for the first time an address of 221 Baker Street existed – but not for long. In 1932 the whole terrace was demolished to make way for Abbey House, the new head offices of the Abbey Road Building Society, later Abbey National.

So, which house did Arthur Conan Doyle have in mind? Gray Chandler Briggs asked the author outright, but he side-stepped the issue by claiming facetiously that he had never set foot in Baker Street. In all probability he was gamely attempting to protect the current residents from being besieged by gawpers who wanted to find out if Sherlock Holmes was in and receiving visitors.

Briggs and many other scholars attempted to identify the site by means of topography, study of architecture and local history. Here are the main candidates, with today's numbering:

Gray Chandler Briggs	111 Baker Street
	(118 as The Empty House)
James Edward Holroyd	109 Baker Street
	(108 as The Empty House)
Vincent Starrett	66 Baker Street
Gavin Brend	61 Baker Street
Heather Owen	53 Baker Street
T.S. Blakeney	49 Baker Street
Bernard Davies	31 Baker Street
	(34 as The Empty House)
Dr Maurice Campbell	27 Baker Street

| Sir Harold Morris | 21 Baker Street |
| James T. Hyslop | 19 Baker Street |

Damage in the Second World War and modern redevelopment have wiped away many of the original buildings on these sites. However, the mews behind Bernard Davies's choice for the Empty House (No. 34) between Blandford Street and George Street is still intact, and it is possible to retrace Holmes and Watson's trail on their way to apprehend Colonel Sebastian Moran.

For detailed accounts of how some of the scholars arrived at their choices, including helpful photographs and maps, we recommend the following sources:

- *Back to Baker Street*, edited by the present authors (includes Bernard Davies's 'The Back Yards of Baker Street' and 'The Mews of Marylebone' and Heather Owen's 'Baker Street Revisited')
- *Sherlock Holmes by Gas-Lamp* edited by Philip A. Shreffler (includes 'The Problem of Number 221' by William S. Baring-Gould)
- *My Dear Holmes: A Study in Sherlock* by Gavin Brend
- *Baker Street By-Ways* by James Edward Holroyd

For more books on the topography of the world of Holmes and Watson, see the Bibliography and Recommended Reading section.

'I HAVE MY EYE ON A SUITE OF ROOMS IN BAKER STREET THAT WILL SUIT US DOWN TO THE GROUND.'

One of the peculiarities of Sherlockians is their love of tangible elements of the world of Sherlock Holmes. Many enthusiasts, for example, have attempted to recreate the 221B sitting room within their own homes, in full size or in miniature.

Throughout the stories, Conan Doyle provided ample information about the furnishings, layout and décor, even going so far as to name some of the books on Holmes and Watson's shelves. We know of the armchairs flanking the fireplace, the basket chair, the settee for visitors, the writing desk, the deal-topped chemical table, the bearskin rug, the sideboard on which rested the gasogene and the tantalus for libations, the pipe-rack, Mrs Hudson's offerings of meals, and, on the occasion of 'The Blue Carbuncle', Henry Baker's lost goose. With this amount of detail, it's no wonder that within our own imaginations we feel so at home and Holmes and Watson seem so real.

Some of the contents of the room inform us even further about the personalities of its inhabitants. In the opening of 'The Musgrave Ritual' Watson famously remarks:

An anomaly which often struck me in the character of my friend Sherlock Holmes was that, although in his methods of thought he was the neatest and most methodical of mankind, and although he affected a certain quiet primness of dress, he was none the less in his personal habits one of the most untidy men that ever drove a fellow lodger to distraction. Not that I am in the least conventional in that respect myself. The rough-and-tumble of work in Afghanistan, coming on the top of a natural Bohemianism of disposition, has made me rather more lax than befits a medical man. But with me there is a limit, and when I find a man who keeps his cigars in the coal scuttle, his tobacco in the toe end of a Persian slipper, and his unanswered correspondence transfixed by a jack-knife into the very centre of his wooden mantelpiece, then I begin to give myself virtuous airs. I have always held, too, that pistol practice should distinctly be an open-air pastime; and when Holmes in one of his queer humours would sit in an arm-chair, with his hair-trigger and a hundred Boxer cartridges, and proceed to adorn the opposite wall with a patriotic V.R. done in bullet-pocks, I felt strongly that neither the atmosphere nor the appearance of our room was improved by it.

Watson makes his own contributions to the assemblage with his pictures of General Gordon and Henry Ward Beecher and his enthusiasm for 'the fine sea stories' of William Clark Russell, and informs us that his cheque book is kept locked in the drawer of Holmes's desk.

Ernest Short, theatre critic and Sherlockian, used the text of the stories to draw a floor plan of the rooms at Baker Street for the March 1950 issue of *The Strand Magazine*. Julian Wolff's interpretation is reproduced in *The Sherlockian Atlas*, and Russell Stutler's can be seen on his website at www.stutler. cc/other/misc/baker_street.html.

'PRAY BE PRECISE AS TO DETAILS.'

Countless variations of the sitting room have appeared in illustrations and film, television and stage productions. Certain early films suggest that Holmes and Watson live in an expensive bordello instead of a thrifty and rather untidy bachelor pad. Some designers must have been making allowance for the large old-style movie cameras, since the room's dimensions often appeared almost palatial. Even more recent versions have over-enthusiastically opted for high Victorian opulence, forgetting that Holmes and Watson had (presumably) limited budgets and little interest in interior design. Like most young men of any era, they wanted comfort, convenience and, basically, just a place to hang out together.

One of the earliest accurate reproductions of 221B was part of the 1951 Festival of Britain, with a Sherlock Holmes exhibition mounted at Abbey House in Baker Street. The late Ronald Searle, renowned for his superb illustrations and cartoons, did a splendid drawing of this version of 221B for *Punch*. Designed by Michael Weight and assembled with the assistance of a group of Holmes aficionados, the exhibit was installed in 1957 at The Sherlock Holmes public house at 10–11 Northumberland Street, London. The footprint of the sitting room is approximately half its original size, but all the important landmarks are present. Diners in the restaurant can view it through the plate-glass window that replaces the fourth wall of the room. There are also viewing windows in the door and corridor alongside the room and the patio area.

Time travel! Steven Moffatt and Sue Vertue, who brought us a twenty-first-century Sherlock Holmes, in the nineteenth-century sitting room at The Sherlock Holmes pub in London. *Photo copyright Jean Upton*

A near duplicate of the 1951 sitting room can also be seen in the Sherlock Holmes Museum at Lucens, near Lausanne in Switzerland, assembled by Adrian Conan Doyle with help from the same designer. Originally housed in the Château de Lucens, the museum reopened in 2001 at the Red House in the town centre.

⸻

In the early 1980s, researchers for Granada Television's Sherlock Holmes series went through all sixty stories, noting every tiny detail. Their dossier served as a reference source for the designers of the sets and costumes, as well as providing key character points for the scriptwriters and actors. This was eventually published as *The Baker Street File* and has continued to be a valuable resource for scholars, authors, and theatre groups.

Some radical changes were made from what one might have expected to see: plain brown paper was used on the walls instead of the traditional busy Victorian wallpaper, and the mirror that would ordinarily hang over the fireplace was replaced with a lithograph of the Reichenbach Falls – partially to avoid the possibility of seeing the reflection of the cameraman, but also as a subtle omen of things to come.

The Sherlock Holmes Museum in Meiringen, Switzerland, houses the most ambitious reconstruction ever achieved. The project was commissioned by Anthony Howlett, who worked with architect John Reid and local Swiss architect Arthur Reinhard. Extensive research ensured that the sitting room

Jeremy Brett on the Granada TV set in December 1987, during a break in shooting *Wisteria Lodge*. *Photo copyright Jean Upton*

was accurate in every detail, right down to the dimensions of the room and even the size of the floorboards. Many of the items in it were donated or loaned by members of the Sherlock Holmes Society of London.

Located in the public square, now known as Conan Doyle Place, the museum is housed in the former English church. It was opened officially in 1991 by Dame Jean Conan Doyle in a ceremony that included Sherlockians from around the world.

An intriguing modern take on the 221B sitting room features in the BBC TV series *Sherlock*. The familiar basic layout of the room has been dressed cleverly with contemporary furniture that, in its 'lived-in' condition, nicely echoes its Victorian counterparts. The naff 1970s wallpaper, emulating nineteenth-century patterns, adds to the illusion of another age. Sherlock Holmes's unanswered correspondence is still jackknifed to the centre of the mantelpiece, but this is a non-smoking environment, so there are no cigars in the coal scuttle or tobacco in a Persian slipper. The emergency stash of cigarettes is secreted in a human skull.

As one would expect, the red Turkey carpet is littered with books and papers. The sleek settee is a favourite place for a supine Holmes to mull over a 'three patch problem'. The 'patriotic V.R. done in bullet-pocks' is replaced by an uncharacteristically cheerful 'smiley face' logo, spray painted onto the wall in acid yellow and peppered with derisory pistol shots. Patriotism is expressed more subtly with the presence of a Union Jack cushion.

Watson's writing desk has been transmogrified into a laptop computer. The kitchen table now doubles as the 'deal-topped chemical table', and it is not unusual for the microwave or the refrigerator to contain unexpected grisly experiments.

There is one fixed point in a changing age: Mrs Hudson still provides ministrations of tea and biscuits, but rightly reminds her lodgers: 'I'm not your housekeeper, dear.'

Yes, this is a twenty-first-century 221B that we can believe in. Full marks to the designers.

We can't even begin to imagine how many miniature versions of 221B have been constructed. If you are looking for ideas, or simply want to be amazed by sheer devotion and craftsmanship, we recommend a visit to the website of the Mini-Tonga Society, named after the diminutive Andaman islander in *The Sign of Four*. Dorothy Rowe Shaw, one of the society's founders, lovingly created a miniature for her husband's collection, and it is now part of the holdings at the University of Minnesota: http://minitonga.thing.com/minitonga2/Mini2.htm

11

'I'M A BELIEVER IN
THE GENIUS LOCI'

• CANONICAL LOCATIONS •

FOR OBVIOUS REASONS, BRITISH Sherlockians have the advantage, if they wish, of being able to follow in the footsteps of Sherlock Holmes. Many of the places featured in the stories are mentioned under their real names, but others are more or less lightly disguised. Most of these have been identified by scholars – through research and sometimes a stretch of the imagination – though it's rare for an identification to be universally accepted. (Lord Donegall, long-time editor of *The Sherlock Holmes Journal*, said: 'The first objective of every aspiring Higher Critic should be *to prove beyond all reasonable doubt* that every preceding Higher Critic had little idea what he was talking about.')

Many of the specific locations, particularly in London, have disappeared, either because of damage sustained during the Second World War, or through the continual modernisation of the city. The Holborn Restaurant, St James's Hall and the Imperial Theatre are long gone. The Café Royal in Regent Street, frequented by aristocrats, bohemians and decadents alike, closed in 2008, and the site is being redeveloped as a luxury hotel. Other sites have been altered through the years, but they do still exist. The main line and underground railway stations, although modernised, are still in operation, and in many cases the original Victorian features have been preserved. Covent Garden Market, long famous for fruit and vegetables, was successfully converted in the 1980s and now houses a wide variety of shops and restaurants. And you can still recognise the building that housed the Turkish baths in Northumberland Avenue.

In 'The Adventure of the Resident Patient', Holmes asks Watson: 'What do you say to a ramble through London?' Happily, for those who wish to join them, much of their world survives.

⚬⊙⚬

Starting at the Lyceum Theatre, where, in *The Sign of Four*, Mary Morstan was instructed to wait by 'the third pillar from the left', you can take a stroll along the Strand to enjoy 'something nutritious at Simpson's'. From that famous restaurant, make for Charing Cross station, and then down Northumberland Street, calling in at The Sherlock Holmes pub for a drink and a look at the preserved head of the Hound of the Baskervilles and other memorabilia, before heading for the Embankment, and perhaps embarking on a river cruise in the wake of the steam launch *Aurora*.

The Criterion at Piccadilly Circus, where Watson and Stamford refreshed themselves at the Long Bar, has been through several different owners and renovations over the years, but the exterior is remarkably unchanged. Nearby in Haymarket is the Theatre Royal, where Josiah Amberley claimed to have gone on the evening of his wife's disappearance.

In the City of London, near the Central Criminal Court at the Old Bailey (which, curiously, is never mentioned in Dr Watson's accounts), much of St Bartholomew's Hospital looks as it did in the days when it was frequented by Holmes, Watson and Stamford. In the hospital's museum, a brass plaque commemorates the historic beginning of a remarkable friendship.

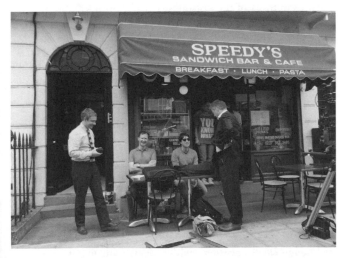

Speedy's café in North Gower Street. Martin Freeman, executive producer Mark Gatiss, director Toby Haynes and Rupert Graves relax before the day's shoot begins, July 2011. *Photo copyright Jean Upton*

Music lovers can still enjoy concerts at the Royal Albert Hall or 'a Wagner night at Covent Garden' and most of the London theatres have retained their opulent Victorian and Edwardian facades and interiors.

Starting from Baker Street, the more energetic may follow the trail of the Blue Carbuncle to 'the Alpha Inn, near the Museum', where Holmes complimented Mr Windigate on his beer. The Museum Tavern and The Plough both have a claim to be the 'real' Alpha Inn. Close by is Montague Street, where Holmes had rooms when he first came up to London.

Twenty-first-century additions to the trail must include North Gower Street, which stands in for Baker Street in BBC's *Sherlock*. Enjoy lunch or a snack at Speedy's café, which features in most of the episodes.

―・◦◦◦・―

We could fill a book with suggestions – but that would be rather silly, as such books already exist. The best of them, we think, are: *Hot on the Scent: A Visitor's Guide to the London of Sherlock Holmes* by Arthur M. Alexander; *The London of Sherlock Holmes* by Thomas Bruce Wheeler, which is ideally used in its e-book format where the map references are hyperlinked to Google Maps and over 400 photographs; *Close to Holmes* by Alistair Duncan, which covers Arthur Conan Doyle's London connections as well as Sherlock Holmes's; and *Sherlock Holmes's London* by David Sinclair.

Allan Foster spreads his net more widely in *Sherlock Holmes and Conan Doyle Locations*, which deals with sites in Scotland and England. Visitors to Devon may wish to consult *The Hound of the Baskervilles: Hunting the Dartmoor Legend* by Philip Weller.

Bernard Davies (1923–2010) was perhaps the world's leading expert on the topography of Sherlock Holmes. His splendid two-volume *Holmes and Watson Country: Travels in Search of Solutions*, in which he identifies sites in London and elsewhere, is Sherlockian scholarship at its very best.

North Americans have rather slim pickings, with only scattered references to various cities or regions in the stories. True, many towns and cities boast a Sherlock Holmes pub, bar or restaurant, and the Baker Street Irregulars have made pilgrimages to the Pennsylvania mining country – the 'Vermissa Valley' of *The Valley of Fear* – and to Salt Lake City. But there is one particular gem of Sherlockiana; the former home of actor William Gillette, which often plays host to meetings of the Men on the Tor, a scion society of the Baker Street Irregulars.

William Gillette's popular portrayal of Sherlock Holmes earned him in excess of $3 million – an enormous amount of money at the time. About one third of it was spent on the most opulent of his whims, Gillette Castle, in East Haddam, Connecticut, built to his own design, along with its ingenious and often highly eccentric fittings. In his will Gillette directed his executors to ensure that the things he loved 'would not fall into possession of some blithering saphead who had no conception of where he is or with what surrounded'. His wishes were observed, as today his property forms the 184-acre Gillette Castle State Park.

In the dusk the castle rises out of the mist, almost appearing to float above the Connecticut River. Twenty-five men toiled

Gillette Castle. A recreation of Sherlock Holmes's study is just one of the remarkable features of William Gillette's eccentric mansion.
Courtesy of Kevin Pepin (released into the public domain by the author)

for five years to complete the main structure: a chunky, eccentric pile of local fieldstone, patterned after a mediaeval fortress.

Upon entering, one progresses upstairs where a welcoming fire awaits in what was Gillette's living room. Possibly influenced by Benjamin Franklin's invention, the Busybody, Gillette had several windowpanes set with mirrors so that he could monitor the movements of his guests unobserved from his upstairs quarters, before coming down to join them.

The twenty-four-room structure has forty-seven doors within, no two exactly the same and each with an intricately carved external latch. Most of the inner décor and furnishings are of hand-hewn white oak, including massive wooden levers, which control the lighting. Sharp eyes will readily note Gillette's fascination with cats; they abound as bookends, figurines and other curios throughout the house. In an upstairs display case is a small black cat, a toy that Gillette used to attach to his favourite hat. There is also the dinner bell employed to summon the multitude of resident cats who, wearing bells on their collars, would speedily congregate for mealtimes. The Victorian artist Louis Wain, also a cat lover, produced a caricature of Gillette as Sherlock Holmes, but re-imagined as a cat in Holmes's dressing gown, holding a revolver in the curve of its serpentine tail.

One room is dedicated to Gillette's love of the river: the Aunt Polly Room is named after his beloved houseboat and contains many items from the vessel. Secreted at the top of a small staircase is Gillette's interpretation of the sitting room at 221B Baker Street. Small but sentimental, it bears a close resemblance to the display at The Sherlock Holmes Pub. At various locations in the house several display cases contain memorabilia from his many years of playing Holmes on the stage, including extremely rare programmes, posters and photographs.

Gillette Castle, 67 River Road, East Haddam,
Connecticut 06423, USA
(860) 526 2336; www.friendsofgillettecastle.org

12

'IT REALLY IS RATHER LIKE ME, IS IT NOT?'

• STATUES •

There was no mistaking the poise of the head, the square-ness of the shoulders, the sharpness of the features… It was a perfect reproduction of Holmes. So amazed was I that I threw out my hand to make sure that the man himself was standing beside me. He was quivering with silent laughter.

'Well?' said he.

'Good heavens!' I cried. 'It is marvellous.'

'The Adventure of the Empty House'

In 'The Empty House', Holmes uses a wax bust of himself, sculpted by M. Oscar Meunier of Grenoble, to lure Colonel Sebastian Moran into the hands of the police. A reproduction of the bust was made for the 1951 Festival of Britain, but this was by no means the first graven image of Sherlock Holmes to go on public display.

ENGLAND

On the façade of the former Saville Theatre in Shaftesbury
Avenue, between Cambridge Circus and High Holborn,
is a sculpted frieze representing drama through the ages,
the work of Gilbert Bayes. The theatre is now a cinema (the
Odeon Covent Garden) but the frieze, carved in 1931,
survives, and there at the turn of the twentieth century is
Sherlock Holmes, staring defiantly at a dramatically menacing
Professor Moriarty. This, we believe, is the first public sculp-
ture of the great detective. (Some wags have suggested that
the gentleman at the end of the row, chatting with one of the
dancing girls, is Dr Watson.)

Sherlock Holmes and
Professor Moriarty face
off. The figures on the
façade of the Odeon
Covent Garden are the
first public sculptures
of the Great Detective
and his arch enemy. *Photo
copyright Roger Johnson*

Why didn't London have its own standalone monument to the Great Detective? The idea was suggested over a century ago, and in 1927, G.K. Chesterton, creator of Father Brown, wrote: 'I hope to see the day when there shall be a statue of Sherlock Holmes in Baker Street.'

In the end the Sherlock Holmes Society of London accepted the challenge, taking advantage of John Doubleday's experience in creating the statue in Meiringen and of the 150th anniversary of the Abbey National, whose premises in Baker Street had housed the seminal Sherlock Holmes Exhibition in 1951. The Sherlock Holmes Statue Company Ltd was set up as the organiser and fundraiser, and Abbey National agreed to cover most of the expense. There was no available site in Baker Street itself,

John Doubleday's statue of Sherlock Holmes at Baker Street station. *Photo copyright Roger Johnson*

so the statue was placed outside the main entrance to Baker Street station in Marylebone Road. The unveiling by Lord Tugendhat on 23 September 1999 was part of a week-long festival that attracted enthusiasts from all over the world – though it was not without incident. At the crucial moment the cloth cover caught on Holmes's pipe and wouldn't budge until John Doubleday leapt up onto the plinth and freed it, amid a burst of laughter and applause. 'The Great Detective' is now an established landmark, and greets visitors as they emerge from the station. Incidentally, the statue was placed facing the station rather than the street so that tourists attempting to take a photograph wouldn't get mown down by passing traffic.

SCOTLAND

As a memorial to Arthur Conan Doyle, the Federation of Master Builders commissioned a statue to be sited in Picardy Place in Edinburgh, a stone's throw from the author's birthplace. The subject was not Conan Doyle himself, however, but Sherlock Holmes. The Sherlock Holmes Society was one of several bodies that contributed money towards the project, and Gerald Laing's splendid statue was duly unveiled on 24 June 1991. Alas, it was taken down in 2009 to make way for the city's new tram system, and is currently in storage. No announcement has yet been made as to where it will be re-sited. Gerald Laing incorporated an artistic joke in homage to the surrealist painter René Magritte: around the bowl of Holmes's pipe is inscribed *'Ceci n'est pas un pipe'*. Quite. Like Magritte's painting, it is only an image of a pipe.

SWITZERLAND

On 10 September 1988 in Meiringen, Switzerland – the village where Holmes and Watson stayed before making their way to the Reichenbach Falls – John Doubleday's life-sized seated statue of Sherlock Holmes was unveiled. It was deliberately designed to encourage visitors to touch it and examine it closely. The sculptor announced that scattered over the statue were clues to each of the sixty stories, and that the first person to identify them all would win a prize. Three years later, after the official opening of the Sherlock Holmes Museum, John Doubleday presented a bronze maquette of the statue to young Michael Meer, who had clocked up a perfect score.

ITALY

The Italian Sherlock Holmes Society (Uno Studio in Holmes) commissioned a very fine bronze bust of Sherlock Holmes by Giancarlo Buratti. It was unveiled in 2002 at Sesto Fiorentino railway station in Florence, Italy, by the mayor, Andrea Barducci, and in 2010 it was moved to the town library, Biblioteca Ernesto Ragionieri, at Piazza della Biblioteca, 4, 50019, Sesto Fiorentino.

RUSSIA

In 2007 a splendid life-size statue of both Holmes and Watson was unveiled on the Smolenskaya embankment near the British Embassy in Moscow. The likenesses, by Andrei Orlov, are actually of the actors Vasily Livanov and Vitaly Solomin, who took the roles in a classic Russian television series. Vasily Livanov was present at the unveiling, as was the British ambassador, Anthony Brenton, who had presented him with his honorary MBE the year before.

JAPAN

The enthusiasm of the Japanese for Sherlock Holmes is unsurpassed. In 1988 the Japan Sherlock Holmes Club commissioned Satoh Yohinori to create a statue of the detective as a memorial to the distinguished translator Ken Nobuhara. It stands in a small park in Karuizawa Town, a highland resort about 80 miles from Tokyo, and was unveiled on 9 October 1988, just a month after the statue in Meiringen.

SIR ARTHUR CONAN DOYLE

Sir Arthur Conan Doyle himself has been immortalised in a life-sized bronze statue at Cloke's Corner in Crowborough, where he spent his last twenty-three years. Until her death in 1997, his daughter Dame Jean worked closely with the sculptor, David Cornell, to ensure an accurate likeness. The unveiling on 14 April 2001 by Georgina Doyle, widow of Sir Arthur's nephew, Brigadier John Doyle, was attended by guests from around the world, including a representative of the Japan Sherlock Holmes Club. Brian Pugh, curator of the Conan Doyle (Crowborough) Establishment, spoke about Conan Doyle's happy years as a resident of Crowborough.

David Cornell's statue of Sir Arthur Conan Doyle in Crowborough. Gyles Brandreth and Roger Johnson pay homage while filming for a television documentary, September 2009.
Photo copyright Roger Johnson

• Plaques •

A NUMBER OF PRIVATELY commissioned plaques may be viewed around London and elsewhere, commemorating incidents in the canon. Heritage plaques granted by English Heritage (blue) or by the local government authority, such as Westminster Council (usually green), indicate connections with Sir Arthur Conan Doyle.

THE CRITERION, PICCADILLY CIRCUS, LONDON W1J 9HP

A circular bronze plaque was unveiled on 3 January 1953 by Chief Inspector Robert Fabian of Scotland Yard and Carleton Hobbs, radio's Sherlock Holmes. Beneath it was another small plaque reading: 'Erected by the Baritsu Chapter of the Baker Street Irregulars, Tokyo'. These plaques, on the outside wall of the building, have disappeared, but in 1981 another was put up inside the restaurant by the Inverness Capers of Akron, Ohio, on behalf of the Sherlock Holmes Society of London and the Baker Street Irregulars. It reads: 'This plaque commemorates the historic meeting early in 1881 at the original Criterion long bar of Dr. Stamford and Dr. John H. Watson which led to the introduction of Dr. Watson to Mr. Sherlock Holmes.'

St Bartholomew's Hospital (Bart's), London EC1A 7BE

Yet another Sherlockian group provided the plaque that commemorates the beginning of Holmes and Watson's historic friendship: 'At this place New Year's Day, 1881 were spoken these deathless words "You have been in Afghanistan, I perceive" by Mr. Sherlock Holmes in greeting to John H. Watson, M.D. at their first meeting. The Baker Street Irregulars – 1953 by the Amateur Mendicants at the Caucus Club.'

The plaque was originally in the pathology laboratory where the meeting took place, but is now easily accessible in the hospital's museum.

Baker Street, London NW1 6XE

In 1985 a plaque on Abbey House was unveiled by the actor Jeremy Brett to identify the important address of 221B Baker Street. Abbey National was taken over by another bank a few years ago and has vacated the building, which is now a luxury apartment block. The plaque has disappeared and its location is currently unknown.

MEIRINGEN, SWITZERLAND

In November 1952 W.T. Rabe of the Old Soldiers of Baker Street arranged for a plaque to be installed at the Rössli Inn in Meiringen, identified by him as the Englischer Hof, where Holmes and Watson stayed. It reads as follows (yes, the name 'Moriarty' is misspelt):

To this valley in May, 1891 came Dr. Watson and Sherlock Holmes and here Holmes bested the infamous Prof. Moriarity in mortal combat: though Holmes was thought to have perished, he escaped and returned to London in 1894. He has since retired to Sussex and bee-keeping.

Current thought favours the Parkhotel du Sauvage, the favourite of British visitors in Victorian and Edwardian times, as the Englischer Hof. A brass plate by the front door reads:

In this hotel, called by Sir Arthur Conan Doyle the
ENGLISCHER HOF
Mr. Sherlock Holmes and Dr. Watson spent the night of
3rd/4th May 1891.
It was from here that Mr. Holmes left for the fatal encounter at the Reichenbach Falls with Professor Moriarty, the Napoleon of Crime.

At the bottom of the funicular railway, where one ascends to view the Reichenbach Falls, is a memorial, which reads:

Across this 'dreadful cauldron' occurred the culminating
event in the career of Sherlock Holmes, the world's greatest detective, when on May 4, 1891 he vanquished Prof.
Moriarty the Napoleon of Crime.

Erected by the Norwegian Explorers of Minnesota and
the Sherlock Holmes Society of London 25 June 1957

The ledge where the fatal struggle took place was identified
by Tony Howlett in 1948. The white star that has long marked
the site was joined in 1992 by a handsome plaque with an
inscription in English, German and French:

1891–1991
At this fearful place, Sherlock Holmes vanquished
Professor Moriarty, on 4 May 1891.
Erected by The Bimetallic Question of Montréal and
The Reichenbach Irregulars of Switzerland

No. 12 Tennison Road, South Norwood SE25 5RT

A blue English Heritage plaque was placed here in 1973 to mark
the house where Arthur Conan Doyle lived from 1891 to 1894.

No. 2 Upper Wimpole Street, London W1G 6LD

The Arthur Conan Doyle Society arranged for a green
Westminster City Council heritage plaque to mark the building where Sir Arthur had his short-lived ophthalmology

practice in 1891. It was unveiled by his daughter Dame Jean on 22 May 1994, Conan Doyle's 135th birthday.

THE LANGHAM HOTEL, PORTLAND PLACE, LONDON W1B 1JA

A joint project of the Sherlock Holmes Society of London, the Oscar Wilde Society and the City of Westminster led to the installation of a green plaque to commemorate the historic dinner held at the Langham by the publisher of *Lippincott's Magazine*, to which Arthur Conan Doyle and Oscar Wilde were invited. The plaque was unveiled on 19 March 2010 by Gyles Brandreth, author of the Oscar Wilde Murder Mysteries, and Councillor Robert Davis. Had the dinner not taken place, there might not have been a second Sherlock Holmes story – a sobering thought.

BAKER STREET UNDERGROUND STATION, LONDON NW1 5LA

Passengers alighting at Baker Street know immediately where they are. The tiled walls of the Bakerloo Line platforms bear large silhouettes of Sherlock Holmes, each composed of hundreds of tiny silhouettes. On the Jubilee Line, the wall of each platform bears seven superb enlargements, about 6ft long by 4ft high, of black-and-white line illustrations of selected Sherlock Holmes stories. They are the work of Robin Jacques, surely the equal of the great illustrators of *The Strand Magazine* and its contemporaries.

ELSEWHERE

There are other plaques to Conan Doyle in the UK:

- 63 Aston Road North, Birmingham B6 4EA, erected by Birmingham Civic Society
- Bush House, Elm Grove, Southsea, Hampshire PO5 1JH
- 1 Durnford Street, Plymouth PL1 3QA
- Hill House Hotel, Happisburgh, Norfolk NR12 0PW
- Edinburgh Medical School at the University of Edinburgh EH16 4TJ, erected by the University

And around the world:

- 2151 Sacramento Street in San Francisco, California, USA
- Writers' Walk, Circular Quay, Sydney, NSW, Australia

ERRATUM

There has been some confusion and erroneous reporting on the internet and elsewhere regarding the blue plaque on the Sherlock Holmes Museum at 239 Baker Street. This plaque was not awarded by English Heritage or any other official body; it was commissioned and installed by the proprietors of the museum. Moreover, the address of the building is not and never has been 221B. '221B Ltd' is the name of a company registered by the museum's proprietors.

13

'THAT'S WHAT PUZZLES ME, MR HOLMES'

· CANONICAL CONUNDRUMS ·

IN THE INTRODUCTION TO his 1944 book *Sherlock Holmes and Dr. Watson – A Textbook of Friendship*, Christopher Morley observed:

Lest one suppose that explanations are unnecessary, take at random a few examples of casual passages. How many young readers know what is a wax vesta? A gasogene, or a tantalus? a commonplace book? a Crockford? a Bradshaw? A wideawake, or a billycock? A London growler? a penang lawyer? When Holmes says he is going to Doctors' Commons, or has had a letter from a tide-waiter, what does he mean? What was the Pink 'Un that the poultry dealer had in his pocket? ... And what sort of image rises in the young reader's mind when he hears of the friend who was invited 'to come and shoot over his preserves'? The natural visualization would be some mischief on pantry shelves.

Nearly seventy years later, a reader approaching the canon for the first time would also, quite understandably, be puzzled by some of these terms, as well other aspects of the stories. Let's first address the order of Morley's list:

Wax Vesta

A match that could be struck on any suitably rough surface. Britain's most popular 'strike anywhere' match is Swan Vesta, first manufactured in 1883. Vesta was the Roman goddess of the hearth.

Gasogene

An early form of soda siphon consisting of two glass globes, one containing water and the other a mixture of chemicals that reacted to produce carbon dioxide, connected by a glass pipe. The result: sparkling water. For safety, the containers were encased in either wire or wicker-work, since it was not uncommon for the glass to

Gasogene and Seltzogene

explode under the pressure of the gas. The name was also commonly used for the similar and more frequently encountered device, correctly called a Seltzogene.

Tantalus

A lockable device that displays decanters containing alcoholic spirits. The master of the house held the key, thus ensuring that the domestic staff couldn't help themselves to a tipple. The name comes from the Greek myth of Tantalus, who was punished by the Gods by having food and drink forever just out of his reach, and is the origin of the word *tantalise*. There are

Tantalus

several types of lockable spirit cases, but only those made by Betjemann & Son are properly called the Tantalus.

Commonplace Book

It was a popular pastime for ladies and gentlemen to keep a sort of scrapbook of interesting information for later reference, usually clippings from newspapers or magazines, arranged by subject or theme. Holmes kept his books in alphabetical order and referred to them as his 'good old index', remarking 'my collection of M's is a fine one'.

Crockford

Crockford's Clerical Directory, first published in 1858 by John Crockford, is the definitive directory of Anglican clergy in the United Kingdom, with some information about the worldwide Anglican Communion. From 1876 to 1917 it was an annual publication. Today *Crockford* is published every two years.

Bradshaw

George Bradshaw enabled British travellers to plan their journeys when he published *Bradshaw's Railway Time Tables and Assistant to Railway Travelling* in 1839. From 1841 the renamed *Bradshaw's Monthly Railway Guide* became the standard source for train times and general railway information. The last issue was published in 1961.

Wideawake

A low-crowned, broad-brimmed hat, sometimes called a Quaker hat.

Billycock

A bowler hat. The origin of the word 'billycock' is debatable.

London Growler

A four-wheeled carriage, so called because of the noise made by the wheels on the cobbled streets.

Penang Lawyer

A walking stick, formidable when used in self defence. It was usually made of palm wood with the head hollowed out and filled with lead for added weight.

Doctors' Commons

Originally a society of ecclesiastical lawyers, the term was then applied to a building near St Paul's Cathedral where records of marriage licenses, divorces and wills were kept. The archive was transferred to Somerset House in 1874, but Holmes still referred to it by the old name.

Tide Waiter

A customs-house officer, whose duty it was to await the arrival of ships to port, and to ensure the observance of all regulations and revenue laws. He would have had useful knowledge regarding the comings and goings of all ships in his port.

The Pink 'Un

The Sporting Times, a weekly publication noted for its horse-racing coverage and printed on pink paper, was known colloquially as 'the Pink 'Un'. The poultry merchant in 'The Blue Carbuncle' had one in his pocket.

Shoot over his preserves

Wealthy landowners would set aside acreage for the breeding and preservation of small game, such as pheasant, grouse and partridge. Guests who were invited for a day or weekend of shooting on these preserves would be practically guaranteed a brace of birds for the dinner table.

To this list we would like to add **life preserver**. Growing up near the coast of New England, Jean knew life preservers as the large, round, cork-filled flotation devices that were tossed to anyone unfortunate enough to fall into deep water (what Roger, who grew up near the East Anglia coast, knew s a lifebelt). You can understand her puzzlement when, at an

early age, she read in the Sherlock Holmes stories that someone kept a life preserver hidden in his sleeve, and someone
else used one to commit murder. A trip to the dictionary soon
revealed that the reference was to a short, flexible club, the
end weighted with lead – what was later called a blackjack or
cosh. With the grinding poverty suffered by so many in the
city, footpads (muggers) were common even in daylight and
a simple walk in the park, especially if unaccompanied, could
be extremely dangerous. It therefore wasn't unusual even for
ladies to carry a life preserver.

There is also the **dark lantern**, which sounds like an oxy-
moron. It is, in fact, a cleverly designed oil lamp with a
moveable shutter that can block out the light without extin-
guishing the flame. The dark lantern was standard police
equipment, and is mentioned in a number of the stories; in
'The Red-Headed League' the ability to mask the light is crucial during the night-time vigil in the vault of the City and
Suburban bank.

Some un-named characters also crop up in the stories:

The Boots
The servant in a hotel or household who cleaned and pol-
ished everyone's boots. Pedestrians in both town and country
had to cope with horse droppings, mud, dust and puddles,
much to the detriment of their boots and shoes. Footwear was

generally left outside one's bedroom door each evening to be collected by 'the boots' for any necessary ministrations. In a world before rampant consumerism, one had a limited wardrobe and thus took good care of it.

The boy in buttons

Also known as a page, this was generally a young boy serving in a household. His main duties were to answer the door and to announce visitors.

The Commissionaire

A retired military man of good character could become a member of the Corps of Commissionaires, founded in 1859. Commissionaires were recognised as trustworthy, and could be conveniently called upon to perform a number of tasks such as delivering messages or parcels, or running simple errands.

You will probably encounter many other words and phrases that require explanation. Rather inconveniently, modern dictionaries no longer include many of the terms that occur regularly throughout Victorian and Edwardian literature. The internet does provide easy reference, but if you are reading in bed late at night it can be tiresome to have to start up the computer in order to satisfy your curiosity. However, there are a number of books available that can be kept to hand for quick reference. Jack Tracy's *The Encyclopaedia Sherlockiana*, originally published in 1977 but still available, is a useful addition to any library.

• 'IT IS QUITE A THREE-PIPE PROBLEM' •

WE GET ASKED A lot of questions about Sherlock Holmes by journalists, teachers, researchers, schoolchildren working on projects, quizmasters and, generally, people who simply haven't yet got around to reading the books but need a quick answer. Here is a selection:

WHEN WAS SHERLOCK HOLMES'S BIRTHDAY?

His birthday is celebrated on 6 January, but there is nothing in the stories themselves to indicate a specific date. Scholars have noted that Holmes quotes twice from Shakespeare's *Twelfth Night*, whose title refers to the twelfth day after Christmas: 6 January. However, it has been suggested that BSI founder Christopher Morley settled on the date because his brother Felix was born on 6 January 1894 – exactly forty years after Sherlock Holmes. Possibly.

The Sherlock Holmes Society of London and the Baker Street Irregulars in New York have always held their annual dinners as near to this date as possible. In recent years, however, a number of people expressed an interest in being able to attend both events, so the two organisations co-operate by holding their dinners one week apart, alternating first and second place.

WAS SHERLOCK HOLMES A COCAINE ADDICT?

Emphatically, no! This is a myth perpetuated in films, plays and pastiche, as it is a useful dramatic device. In the early days Holmes used cocaine on the rare occasions when he did not have a case to occupy his mind, and Watson, as a medical man, was deeply and justifiably concerned over even this infrequent use. Only in *The Sign of Four* is Holmes actually shown as using the drug. There are only passing references in a handful of other cases, and Watson reports in 'The Missing Three-Quarter' that he has managed to wean Holmes off the drug.

During the nineteenth century cocaine was not an illegal drug. It was actually suggested as a cure for alcohol and opium addition and was readily available from chemists – as, rather frighteningly, were opium and arsenic. Cocaine was used quite casually in tea or wine as a 'pick-me-up'. The earliest formulas for a universally popular soft drink included cocaine, and it still bears the name Coca Cola. The drug was fashionable throughout society; even Queen Victoria indulged. Some purveyors offered their customers a convenient starter package of a syringe and a small amount of the drug.

Medical knowledge, especially about the effects of different substances on the body, is constantly evolving. Rather than condemn the Victorians, we should remember that only a few decades ago cigarettes were publicised as healthful and soothing to the throat, and cheerful advertisements in *The Strand Magazine* recommended cigarette gift boxes as Christmas presents.

WAS HOLMES A MISOGYNIST?

Holmes didn't hate women, but he seems never to have been wholly at ease with them. He said himself: 'Women are never to be entirely trusted – not the best of them', and Dr Watson noted: 'He disliked and distrusted the sex, but he was always a chivalrous opponent.' In fact, throughout the recorded adventures he treated most women with the utmost courtesy, whatever their age or rank, from the feather-brained Lady Hilda Trelawney Hope to the prostitute Kitty Winter.

Despite his apparent immunity to feminine beauty, he acknowledged that Irene Adler 'was a lovely woman, with a face that a man might die for', but it was her intelligence that most impressed him. The same is true of Violet Hunter, whom he recognised as 'a quite exceptional woman', and of Maud Bellamy, who, he said, 'possessed strong character as well as great beauty'.

WHAT SORT OF PIPE DID SHERLOCK HOLMES SMOKE?

Most of the stylised images of Sherlock Holmes portray him with a big curly calabash, though there is no mention of such a pipe in any of the stories. The actor William Gillette found that a bent briar was easier to handle on stage than a straight-stemmed pipe (as depicted in Sidney Paget's illustrations for *The Strand Magazine*) and enabled him to deliver his lines unobstructed. The calabash, made from a gourd and lined with meerschaum, seems to have appeared first in an early film comedy.

In Conan Doyle's stories, Holmes is reported to smoke a briar pipe, a black clay (this would be 'the old and oily clay pipe, which was to him as a counsellor'), and a 'long cherry-wood pipe which was wont to replace his clay when he was in a disputatious rather than a meditative mood', but there were certainly others, as Watson mentions 'a litter of pipes' in the detective's bedroom as well as a pipe rack in the sitting room. One of the pipes at least had a stem of 'reeking amber'.

Having an immense knowledge of tobacco, and an appreciation for the different types and blends, Holmes would have reserved a different pipe for a specific tobacco since a pipe will retain the flavour of what has been smoked in it.

The black clay pipe has caused some debate amongst scholars. Some years ago, when several London tobacconists were asked, they all denied that such a thing existed. The theory was that Holmes smoked a white clay pipe that had become blackened from tar, soot and natural oils that transfer from one's skin. Today, however, a quick whiz around the internet indicates that a black clay pipe did exist and was popular in the seventeenth century. A German company has continued to make them, and a business in Devon now makes reproductions of the seventeenth-century style that might appeal to collectors (www.dawnmist.demon.co.uk/pipesale.htm). Of course, the question still remains as to whether Holmes smoked a black clay or a *blackened* clay pipe…

WHAT WAS SHERLOCK HOLMES'S FAVOURITE FOOD?

No particular favourite is specified in the stories. In *The Sign of Four* Holmes and Watson dine on oysters and a brace of grouse with white wine. In 'A Scandal in Bohemia' Holmes settles for cold roast beef and beer. In 'The Blue Carbuncle' Mrs Hudson is preparing a woodcock for dinner. In 'The Veiled Lodger' there is 'a cold partridge on the sideboard' and a bottle of Montrachet. Breakfast at 221B seems to have been straightforward ham and eggs, though in 'The Naval Treaty' Percy Phelps is also offered curried chicken.

After he starves himself to feign illness in 'The Dying Detective', Holmes suggests that 'something nutritious at Simpson's would not be out of place'. Simpson's is still renowned for generous portions of roast beef and Yorkshire pudding and other joints of roast meat, which are wheeled out under huge domes by attentive waiters and are carved expertly at tableside.

Anyone desiring to prepare a meal that might have graced the table of 221B should peruse *Dining with Sherlock Holmes: A Baker Street Cookbook* by Julia Rosenblatt and Frederic Sonnenschmidt. Patricia Guy's *Bacchus at Baker Street: Sherlock Holmes &Victorian Drinking Lore* provides details on the preferred tipples of the residents and guests of 221B.

WHY DID SHERLOCK HOLMES ALWAYS WEAR A DEERSTALKER?

He didn't. The deerstalker isn't even mentioned in the stories. Holmes dressed as a typical gentleman of his day. His headgear would have been chosen as appropriate to the occasion. For daily wear around London, a bowler, fedora or silk topper would have been the norm. Evening dress, especially when going to the theatre or concert hall, would have called for an opera hat.

Journeys out of the city and into the countryside were entirely another matter. This was the age of steam, and travel by train meant that one was inevitably engulfed in clouds of smoke, grit, grime and hot cinders. Equally, if travelling by road, carriage wheels would throw up the ever-present horse manure as well as dust when the weather was dry and mud when the weather was wet. Regardless of the method of transport, a sturdy travelling cloak and hat were in order if one was to preserve one's suit of clothing and ward off any inclement weather.

Conan Doyle mentions a 'close-fitting cloth cap' and an 'ear-flapped travelling-cap', which Sidney Paget interpreted as a deerstalker in his illustrations, partly because he wore one himself. Its design makes a very pleasing profile, and so the popular image has stuck.

WAS THERE MORE THAN ONE LANDLADY OF 221B BAKER STREET?

Mrs Hudson is the landlady throughout the stories. In 'A Scandal in Bohemia' there is an accidental mention of a Mrs Turner. This was a lapse on the part of Conan Doyle, who made the same error in the original manuscript of 'The Empty House', but corrected it to read Mrs Hudson. Some writers have cleverly picked up on this little detail. In Steven Moffat's script for 'A Study in Pink' in the BBC series *Sherlock*, Mrs Hudson mentions: 'Mrs Turner, next door'.

WERE HOLMES AND WATSON GAY?

It's unlikely. The idea appears to have first arisen about fifty years ago, and lazy journalists with no knowledge of social history resurrect it for a quick and easy story whenever there is a new dramatic adaptation. The theory has no firmer basis than the fact that two unmarried men were sharing a flat.

Here's a thought to put things in perspective: until the early twentieth century, a man who needed accommodation at a country inn or public house would not only be expected to share a room, but would more than likely be expected to share the bed with a complete stranger.

Living in London, or any major city, is, and always has been, expensive. The options for someone on a straitened budget were limited. They could settle for a depressingly dingy room in a boarding house or a residential hotel, or take a room in a family household, which might be affordable, but could be inconvenient and even hazardous. The most attractive proposition, however, would have been to share a flat with another person of one's own choice, which offered the independence to come and go whenever one wished without having to adhere to 'house rules'.

In the 1880s 'a suite of rooms in Baker Street', no matter how basic, would have seemed like the height of luxury to two young men attempting to gain a foothold in 'that great cesspool into which all the loungers and idlers of the Empire are irresistibly drained'.

What of the fact that Holmes and Watson sometimes addressed each other as 'my dear'? What they actually said, of course, was 'my dear fellow' or 'my dear Watson', which was common parlance of the time, with 'dear' meaning 'valued'. Our mode of conversation may have changed, but we still begin a letter, even to a stranger, with the word 'dear'.

Putting a different slant on Holmes and Watson's relationship is nothing new. Rex Stout, creator of Nero Wolfe, delivered a paper to the 1941 BSI dinner entitled 'Watson Was a Woman'. It was met with hoots of derision. The following year Julian Wolff delivered his retort 'That Was No Lady'. Since then, entire books have been written on the premise that either Holmes or Watson was a woman.

THE CHRONOLOGY OF SOME OF THE STORIES DOESN'T MAKE SENSE. WHAT'S GOING ON?

This is a minefield that has given rise to countless scholarly papers and discussions. In an interview filmed shortly before his death, Conan Doyle remarked, with a grin, that he got 'letters addressed to his [Holmes's] rather stupid friend, Watson'. In fact, a number of errors appear throughout the stories, mostly attributable to the manner in which Conan Doyle chose to write. More often than not, he was working to a tight deadline, and dealing with numerous interruptions, sometimes carrying on important conversations while writing. And, hard though it may be to accept, he devoted much less care to the details of the Sherlock Holmes stories than he did to his historical novels, which he considered to be much more important.

His mind worked in such a precise manner, with ideas already formed and refined, that his manuscripts reveal surprisingly little in the way of revisions. Although he often read his newly written stories aloud to his family, unless a glaring error was pointed out at that time, the manuscript swiftly went off to the publishers with no further proofreading or amendments.

WHERE WAS WATSON WOUNDED?

In *A Study in Scarlet* Watson states that at the battle of Maiwand he 'was struck on the shoulder by a Jezail bullet, which shattered the bone and grazed the subclavian artery'. However, in *The Sign of Four* he speaks of his wounded leg, saying: 'I had had a Jezail bullet through it some time before, and though it did not prevent me from walking it ached wearily at every change of the weather.' In Sherlockian lore this has come to be known as 'Watson's Wandering Wound'. One imaginative theory put forward in a scholarly paper suggested that, while he was bending over a patient on the battlefield, a bullet passed through his buttock and lodged in the shoulder, thus providing both wounds at once. Unfortunately this ignores Holmes's reference to Watson's 'damaged *tendo Achillis*', otherwise known as the Achilles tendon, which connects the calf muscles to the heel bone.

BBC's *Sherlock* neatly deals with the issue by making John's limp a psychosomatic symptom of post-traumatic stress.

WATSON SAYS HIS FIRST NAME IS JOHN, BUT WHY DOES HIS WIFE CALL HIM JAMES?

This is recorded just once, in 'The Man With the Twisted Lip', and it is another slip of the pen. However, Dorothy L. Sayers put forth the rather charming idea that Watson's second name was Hamish, the Scottish equivalent of James, which his wife might have preferred.

HOW MANY TIMES WAS WATSON MARRIED?

This has been a topic of debate for many years, and will probably never be resolved. We know for certain that Watson was married once, to Mary Morstan, whom he met in *The Sign of Four*. Given Watson's eye for the ladies, it has been argued that Mary was his second wife, but there is no evidence for the idea.

In 'The Empty House' Watson states: 'In some manner he [Holmes] had learned of my own sad bereavement, and his sympathy was shown in his manner rather than in his words.' It's clear that Mary has died, but no information is given as to how she met her death. Because no antibiotics existed for them at the time, influenza, bronchitis and pneumonia contributed regularly to the mortality rate, as did tuberculosis and typhoid. However, as Watson makes no mention of an illness, it is likely that Mary died in childbirth, which was a sadly common occurrence, especially in cases of a difficult delivery, and often with the newborn accompanying its mother in the grave.

It is generally accepted that he married again. In 'The Blanched Soldier', Holmes, writing of events in January 1903, says: 'The good Watson had at that time deserted me for a wife, the only selfish action which I can recall in our association.' This lady is not named, and it has been suggested that she was actually some other man's wife, which might explain the accusation of selfishness. However, most scholars agree that she and Watson did marry, and some insist that there was a third and even fourth Mrs Watson.

At their annual dinner, the Baker Street Irregulars always include a toast to the second Mrs Watson. In 2002 the following toast was given:

> Watson had a second wife
> But, did he lead a double life?
> He had two wounds; he had two names
> (One was John, the other, James).
> He often claimed he dined alone
> Yet quaffed whole bottlesful of Beaune.
> He'd disappear for days on end
> Accompanying his clever friend,
> Then lame excuses where he'd been
> Were published in Strand Magazine.
> And so to the spouse of this pain in the ass
> We raise a toast and lift our glass.

WAS WATSON REALLY A STUPID BUMBLER?

Can you honestly imagine Sherlock Holmes sharing lodgings with a stupid bumbler? This image of Watson as 'Boobus Britannicus' has arisen mainly from Nigel Bruce's portrayal of him in the films with Basil Rathbone and was subsequently picked up by other filmmakers. However, much of that image is the fault of the scripts, which required Watson to do or say something stupid in order to advance the plot.

Going back to the original stories, Watson sometimes appears ingenuous, but this is in order to benefit the reader. He serves as the filter through which we observe Holmes. Without Watson requiring explanations, we would not have the benefit of understanding how Holmes arrived at his deductions.

Holmes does occasionally criticise Watson, but it is friendly chaffing; Holmes knows that Watson's thought processes can't match his, but needs a way of letting out his frustration when an expected solution is not immediately derived.

WHAT'S THE CORRECT PRONUNCIATION OF...?

In the many dramatisations of the stories there has been much debate over the pronunciation of the names of some of the characters.

Let's first deal with Inspector Lestrade. The original French pronunciation of his name would have a broad 'a' as was used in most of the earlier films: 'Le-*straahd*'. However, in conversation with Dame Jean Conan Doyle we learned that her father, when reading aloud to her, always pronounced it with a long 'a': 'Le-*strayed*'. With such impeccable insider knowledge, this is what Jeremy Brett chose to use.

Irene Adler is not quite so clear cut. There is the standard American pronunciation of 'Eye-*reen*', which would be appropriate since she is said to have come from New Jersey. British usage follows the original Greek in pronouncing the final 'e' of the name, thus: 'Eye-*ree*-nee' (as in 'Penelope', 'Hermione' and other names of Ancient Greek origin). The Granada TV

Jeremy Brett and Dame Jean Conan Doyle in J.B.'s dressing-room at Wyndham's Theatre, after the first night of *The Secret of Sherlock Holmes*, 22 September 1988. *Photo copyright Jean Upton*

series opted for a more exotic version – 'Ayr-*ray*-na' – which has a continental flavour fitting for a diva who made her name in the opera houses of Europe. The BBC *Sherlock* series, after considerable deliberation, went for the popular and more modern Eye-*reen*. We leave it to the reader to decide.

Why was Alice Rucastle's hair cut?

In 'The Copper Beeches', Violet Hunter is puzzled and concerned about her employer's insistence that she have her hair cut 'quite short'. It is not until the end of the story that we discover that the intention was that she imperson-ate the Rucastles's daughter, who had been threatened and bullied into serious illness and then held prisoner in the house. Mrs Toller says: 'she got brain fever, and for six weeks was at death's door. Then she got better at last, all worn to a shadow, and with her beautiful hair cut off…'

Was it a punishment? An old wives' tale, with the idea that cutting off the hair would ensure a rapid cure? Was it to facilitate easier bathing of the invalid? It is not made clear in the text of the story.

In order to understand the significance of a young lady of that era having her hair cut off, we need at least a cursory knowledge of the fashions and proprieties of the times. Cosmetics were rarely and sparingly used and a woman's most attractive feature was generally her hair. There were strict guidelines as to when it was appropriate for a young girl to wear her hair up, thus signifying her maturity and availability to be approached by interested males.

It was not unusual for a female of that era to go through her entire life without scissors ever coming near her locks. A contemporary carryover from this tradition is the spirited actress Rosalie Williams, Mrs Hudson of the Granada television series, who once remarked (with understandable pride) that it was not necessary for the wardrobe department to supply her with a wig for the part, as the long hair, artfully styled, was her own.

Getting back to Alice Rucastle, consider that her hair, when not done up, reached her waist, and possibly even down as far as her knees. Although individual strands will blow about in the slightest breeze, such a quantity of hair is surprisingly heavy. Anyone who has experienced a serious illness over a long period of time will recall how physically weak the body becomes. Poor Alice would have struggled to walk upright with the sheer weight of that amount of hair putting a strain on her severely weakened muscles. Try walking around with a damp beach towel wrapped around your head, and you will get some notion of what it must have been like for her. Cutting the hair to chin or shoulder length removed that burden and allowed the invalid to begin to move about more easily during the period of recuperation.

IN WHICH STORY DOES HOLMES SAY 'ELEMENTARY, MY DEAR WATSON'?

The expression does not appear in any of the original stories. Holmes occasionally said 'elementary' or 'my dear Watson' but never as a combined phrase.

It was first used by P.G. Wodehouse in *Psmith, Journalist* in 1915. Then, in 1929 Garrett Fort and Basil Dean included it in their script for the film *The Return of Sherlock Holmes* starring Clive Brook, and it became immovably stuck in the mind of the public. In 1948 an annoyed Humfrey Michell wrote to the *Baker Street Journal*: 'Never did Holmes say "Elementary, my dear Watson!" Let it, therefore, be banished from the vocabulary of all true Irregulars.'

WHEN DOES HOLMES SAY 'QUICK, WATSON – THE NEEDLE'?

This is another apocryphal expression. It's actually a misquotation of the final line of dialogue in the Rathbone and Bruce film, *The Hound of the Baskervilles*: 'Oh, Watson – the needle!'

14

'MOST SINGULAR
AND WHIMSICAL'

• THE GRAND GAME •

IMAGINE A PARALLEL UNIVERSE, in which Holmes, Watson, Mrs Hudson, Inspector Lestrade, Professor Moriarty et al. are real people. Watson writes up Holmes's cases, all of which reflect true historical events, and Arthur Conan Doyle acts as his literary agent. That's the basis for the Grand Game.

Dr Watson was frequently a bit careless in terms of keeping the dates and details straight in his chronicles of the Great Detective. For more than a century this has provided the fodder for countless distinguished scholars to ruminate upon.

Articles about Sherlock Holmes were published as long ago as 1902, when Frank Sidgwick in England and Arthur Bartlett Maurice in America were stimulated by his reappearance in *The Hound of the Baskervilles* to comment on some of the oddities and inconsistencies in the stories. They were, as far as we know, the first to use Holmes's own methods of observation and deduction in examining him and his exploits, but others quickly followed. There were at least five more papers before 1911, when Ronald A. Knox read and then published 'Studies in the Literature of Sherlock Holmes', which many regard as the foundation of the game.

Among the players were some familiar names: A.A. Milne, Dorothy L. Sayers, Rex Stout, Ellery Queen, Vincent Starrett, Anthony Boucher, Basil Rathbone and President Franklin Delano Roosevelt, just to name a few. In her 1946 book *Unpopular Opinions*, Dorothy L. Sayers hailed Ronald Knox as the founder of the game, but added: 'The rule of the game is that it must be played as solemnly as a county cricket match at Lord's: the slightest touch of extravagance or burlesque ruins the atmosphere' – an interesting comment, given that Knox's paper was an admitted spoof, full of jokey names and parodies of cultural stereotypes.

But not everyone understood the game or appreciated the admiration that inspired it. Denis Conan Doyle attended the 1940 dinner of the Baker Street Irregulars and was bewildered by the experience, urgently whispering to Edgar W. Smith: 'I don't understand this! My father's name has not been mentioned.' Smith explained that it was the highest possible compliment any author could wish for: 'No other writer, not even Shakespeare can boast of creating a character so vivid that people believe in the character rather than the author.' Nonetheless, Denis clearly disapproved. His and his brother Adrian's attitude towards the Baker Street Irregulars, and, in fact, anyone else who played the Grand Game, bordered on vitriolic. This is well documented in the archival history of the BSI, and need not be enlarged upon here.

The affection that Sherlockians actually feel for Arthur Conan Doyle is eloquently expressed by Christopher Morley: 'Myself I do not wholly agree with the tradition that A.C.D. should never be formally mentioned. I loved him long before his heirs and assigns and agents were born and I find in his writings the most delicious asymptotes to the Holmes-Watson codex. As I have often said, how ridiculous he was only Knighted – he should have been Sainted.'

Publicly, however, the Baker Street Irregulars maintained for decades, in defiance of his heirs, that Conan Doyle had no part in their world, except as John H. Watson's literary agent.

The Sherlock Holmes Society of London has always been less doctrinaire. In his 1959 book *Baker Street Byways*, James Edward Holroyd said: 'The Sherlockian umbrella is

The Baker Street Irregulars' 1940 annual dinner at the Murray Hill Hotel, New York. 1: Edgar W. Smith. 2: Denis Conan Doyle. 3: Felix Morley. 4: Frederic Dorr Steele. 5: Christopher Morley. 6: Frank V. Morley. *Courtesy of Jon Lellenberg and Bill VandeWater*

big enough to accommodate those aficionados who believe that Dr. Watson wrote the stories as well as those who give the credit to his friend, Sir Arthur Conan Doyle' and nearly thirty years later Anthony Howlett observed: 'I have never seen any problem in reconciling the recognition of the undoubted fact of Doyle's authorship with the undoubted fact of Watsonian authorship according to the Dogma of Absolute Reality.'

Their comments are particularly relevant today, as the Grand Game has been enthusiastically embraced by a team of new, young players inspired by the BBC TV series *Sherlock*. After the episode entitled 'The Reichenbach Fall' was broadcast in the UK, homemade posters appeared in London and elsewhere with the messages: 'I believe in Sherlock Holmes' and 'Moriarty is real'. Since the series first aired, sales of Arthur Conan Doyle's original books have soared and hits on the Sherlock Holmes Society's website shot up, as did membership figures. The Grand Game and the Great Detective are indeed alive and well.

POSTSCRIPT

We should like to add that Dame Jean Conan Doyle, Sir Arthur's youngest child, did not share her brothers' scornful attitude. She was gracious, courteous and supportive, with a wonderful sense of humour. Sympathetic and appreciative of the eccentric ways in which Holmesians honoured her father, she happily attended our annual dinners and even accompanied the pilgrims to Switzerland. We miss her.

15

'YOU HAVE BEEN AT YOUR CLUB ALL DAY'

• THE SHERLOCK HOLMES SOCIETIES •

THE BAKER STREET IRREGULARS

The oldest and longest running society is the Baker Street Irregulars, named after Holmes's gang of street urchins, who 'can go everywhere, see everything, overhear everyone'. The BSI's origins can be traced back to the childhood of its founder, author Christopher Morley (1890–1957), who would read the stories aloud to his younger brothers, Felix and Frank, and then quiz them on the contents. By 1902, Kit Morley and three of his Baltimore school friends had formed what is arguably the first documented Sherlock Holmes society, The Sign of Four. He recounted some of their activities in his entertaining semi-autobiographical novel, *Thorofare*.

By the 1930s, Morley had established a reputation as a newspaper columnist, novelist, poet and general congenial character, who held forth at meetings of the Three Hours for Lunch Club, the Grillparzer Sittenpolizei Verein, and other such organisations, often invented by him at the drop of a hat (or a cocktail glass). Several factors combined to inspire his creation of the Baker Street Irregulars: his commissioning, shortly after Conan Doyle's death in 1930, to write the preface to the Complete Sherlock Holmes published by Doubleday, Doran; William Gillette's 1929–32 farewell tour in his melodrama *Sherlock Holmes*; S.C. Roberts's 1931 monograph *Doctor Watson*; Vincent Starrett's 1933 book *The Private Life of Sherlock Holmes*; and Elmer Davis's review of that book in the *Saturday Review of Literature*.

The founding event of the Baker Street Irregulars was really the Sherlock Holmes birthday party that Morley gave at the Hotel Duane in New York on 6 January 1934. It prompted him to announce a dinner for aficionados on 5 June at Christ Cella's restaurant on East 45th Street, with invitations awarded to those who completed his brother Frank Morley's Sherlockian crossword puzzle, published in Kit's column in the *Saturday Review of Literature*. Interestingly, several women qualified but were not invited; the event was decidedly masculine. Morley's written invitation ended with the lines: 'Dress informally of course. This first meeting will be stag.' The dinner remained a men-only occasion until 1992.

The first annual dinner of the BSI took place on 7 December 1934 at Christ Cella's. Eighteen were present besides Christopher Morley, including the actor William Gillette; illustrator Frederic Dorr Steele; Vincent Starrett; Gray Chandler Briggs, who discovered the real Camden

House in Baker Street and so identified the building opposite as 221B; Robert K. Leavitt, later to write 'The Origin of 221B Worship'; Basil Davenport; journalist Elmer Davis; heavyweight boxing champion Gene Tunney; critic and *New Yorker* columnist Alexander Woollcott; H.W. Bell, whose pioneering chronology influenced Holmes scholars on both sides of the ocean; A.G. Macdonell, co-founder that same year of the British Sherlock Holmes Society; and Laurence P. Dodge.

The following month a constitution was drawn up by Elmer Davis, stating that the society's purpose 'shall be the study of the Sacred Writings'. Officers were stipulated: the Gasogene (president), Tantalus (secretary) and Commissionaire, whose duties were 'to telephone down for ice, White Rock (soda water), and whatever else may be required and available; to conduct all negotiations with waiters; and to assess the members *pro rata* for the cost of same' – allusions to the BSI's gestation in a speakeasy during the Prohibition era.

The accompanying Buy Laws (*sic*) included the drinking of toasts 'after which the members shall drink at will' and the game, intended for the original smaller gatherings, in which a round of drinks must be bought 'by any member who fails to identify, by title of story and context, any quotation from the Sacred Writings submitted by any other member'.

The closing items of the Buy Laws are still gleefully chanted in unison at the modern dinners:

(4) All other business shall be left for the monthly meeting.
(5) There shall be no monthly meeting.

Press reports on these extraordinary dinners resulted in many additional guests as the years passed, which was a far cry from Morley's impromptu gatherings of 'kinsprits' (kindred spirits) where part of the charm was what Robert G. Harris called the 'Disputation, Confrontation, and Dialectical Hullabaloo' that can only be achieved in smaller gatherings.

Enter Edgar W. Smith, a senior executive of General Motors. In 1936 he wrote to Vincent Starrett, having read *The Private Life of Sherlock Holmes* with great enthusiasm. In Starrett's reply, delayed until his return from abroad in 1937, Smith learned of the BSI, which was then temporarily dormant. The hiatus ended in 1940, when Smith started to take an active role. In 1946 he became the first editor of *The Baker Street Journal*, and Sherlockian scholarship burgeoned to such a degree that Morley made the Churchillian comment: 'Never has so much been written by so many for so few.'

Smith continued as head of the Baker Street Irregulars, with the title 'Buttons-cum Commissionaire', until his death in 1960, when Julian Wolff took the reins as 'Commissionaire', then handing over to Thomas Stix, Jr., a second-generation BSI, as 'Wiggins' in 1986. The current 'Wiggins', since 1997, is Michael Whelan.

Attendance at the annual dinner is by invitation only, and limited to invested members and suitable guests, including those being considered for investiture. The proceedings include some delightfully eccentric rituals, some of which have survived from the earliest years:

- A reading of The Constitution and Buy-Laws
- A responsorial recitation of The Musgrave Ritual
- 'Stand With Me Upon the Terrace': Tributes to members who have died during the year
- The singing of 'We Never Mention Aunt Clara'
- The Toasts
- The Investitures: Until this point in the proceedings the identities of the new investitures have been kept a closely guarded secret. Individuals who are recognised in their efforts of 'keeping green the memory of the master' are awarded the name of a person, place or thing mentioned in the Canon. They also receive a handsome document affixed with the Irregular Shilling

Once the dinner has dispersed, informal celebrations tend to carry on until the wee hours of the following morning, especially among the newly invested.

During his tenure as commissionaire, and when the BSI was a much smaller organisation, Julian Wolff generously held an annual cocktail party for Sherlockians at his own apartment, and later, as the invitation list grew, at his club, The Grolier. Today held in much larger premises, the cocktail party has become the Baker Street Irregulars's Annual Reception and is open to 'all Sherlockians and friends'.

The story of the Irregulars, as recounted in the BSI archival histories, makes fascinating reading from both the historical and the literary point of view.

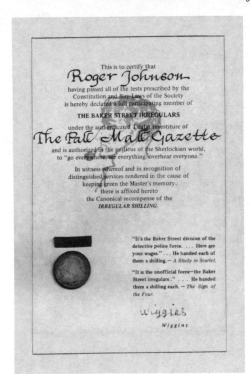

The 'Irregular Shilling'.
Collection of Roger Johnson and Jean Upton

Christopher Morley's centenary was marked in 1990 with the publication of his collected Sherlockian writings in a single volume, *The Standard Doyle Company*, edited by Steven Rothman. *The Complete Sherlock Holmes*, published by Doubleday and later by Penguin, continues to be reprinted with Morley's now legendary preface. Especially worth seeking out is *Sherlock Holmes and Dr. Watson: A Textbook of Friendship*, published in 1944 and notable for being the first annotated collection containing five of the more popular stories.

Although membership to the BSI is limited, there are satellite groups known as Scion Societies all over the United States – in fact, all over the world. More information on these groups follows this section. Additionally, anyone interested may subscribe to *The Baker Street Journal*, which is published four times a year: www.bakerstreetjournal.com

THE ADVENTURESSES OF SHERLOCK HOLMES

From the very beginning, women were just as interested in Sherlock Holmes as men, but although two women – Lenore Glen Offord in 1959 and Lisa McGaw in 1982 – were invested into the Baker Street Irregulars, neither was ever invited to join their *confrères* at the annual dinner in New York. Equal recognition took an inordinate amount of time to achieve. Barred from joining the BSI, a group of young students from Albertus Magnus College in New Haven, Connecticut, took matters into their own hands. It was the 1960s, a time of youth uprisings and protests against injustice; what could be more unjust than the exclusion of women? They had already attracted the sympathetic attention of Holmes biographer and annotator William S. Baring-Gould, eminent Sherlockian friend-of-all-the-world John Bennett Shaw and legendary collector and scholar Peter Blau; confidence in their cause was growing.

So, on the evening of 5 January 1968, a group of six determined young ladies in miniskirts, one with a bandaged foot and a cane, picketed outside Cavanagh's restaurant on West 23rd Street, where the Irregulars were gathering for their

annual dinner. Julian Wolff, the normally genial commissionaire, was incandescent and sought out Shaw, growling: 'Your
damned girls are at the door – do something!' In the absence
of the recently deceased Baring-Gould, Shaw picked up
Blau for support along the way, and a temporary *détente* was
achieved over cocktails. Though still continuing to lobby for
equality, the Adventuresses of Sherlock Holmes (ASH) began
to hold their own annual dinners, and the group flourished
under the auspices of its Principal Unprincipled Adventuress,
Evelyn Herzog. Investitures were bestowed upon its members, who chose their desired name from the canon.

Over the years the dinners continued and various eccentric
rituals evolved, such as the shrill soprano call of '*Laaadies!*'
to begin the formal proceedings. There was good food and
drink, witty entertainment combined with erudition, and
excellent companionship.

At the BSI cocktail party in January 1991, Tom Stix, then
in charge as 'Wiggins', stunned the crowd by announcing an
investiture 'being made simultaneously in England'. It was
awarded to Dame Jean Conan Doyle: 'A Certain Gracious
Lady'. Amid roars of approval the other women invested on
this historic occasion were: Katherine McMahon, only sur-
vivor of the women who had solved the original crossword
puzzle in the *Saturday Review of Literature*; Edith Meiser, who
had adapted the Sherlock Holmes stories for radio; Evelyn
Herzog, founder of the ASH; Julia Rosenblatt, co-author of
Dining with Sherlock Holmes; and noted scholar Susan Rice.

As Susan Rice reported: 'Wiggins had not only unlocked
the door – he had kicked it open! Here was history being

made before our eyes. The BSI was truly open at last. Just to be certain that nobody could misinterpret what had happened this day, Wiggins added, "I want to make it plain that these are full investitures, with all the rights and privileges thereof.'"

Amid great celebration there were heard some isolated masculine howls of contempt, and a few disbelievers were seen to make an early escape from this den of equity.

Since then investiture of women has continued. The lively alternative Holmes birthday dinner founded by ASH is now known as the Gaslight Gala and run by a committee of local Sherlockians; it welcomes both women and men who are not attending the BSI dinner, which is held on the same night.

Having awarded special membership later in 1991 to the men who had been the group's main benefactors, in 2008 the Adventuresses finally opened their membership fully to men as well as women.

During the week of the birthday festivities the ASH also host the ASH Wednesday dinner and an informal Sunday brunch, as well as other events in spring and autumn. Their journal, *The Serpentine Muse*, is published quarterly. Enquiries about the Adventuresses are welcome and should be made in writing to: Evelyn A. Herzog, 301 Warren Avenue, #203, Baltimore, Maryland, USA 21230. Their website is: www. ash-nyc.com

For more detail about the beginnings of ASH, we recommend *The Baker Street Journal* Christmas Annual 2004, *Dubious and Questionable Memories: A History of the Adventuresses of Sherlock Holmes*, edited by Susan Rice.

THE SHERLOCK HOLMES SOCIETY OF LONDON

The first dinner of the original Sherlock Holmes Society was held on 6 June 1934, at Canuto's restaurant in Baker Street. Besides the president, Canon H.R.L. (Dick) Sheppard, and the secretary, writer A.G. Macdonnel, those present included Frank Morley, perpetrator of the Sherlockian crossword puzzle, S.C. Roberts, painter Gerald Kelly, and crime writers Dorothy L. Sayers, Gladys Mitchell, E.R. Punshon and Anthony Berkeley.

Congratulatory messages were received from Vincent Starrett and others, and Morley read 'a cryptic telegram of greeting to the Society from the Gasogene of the Baker Street Irregulars'. R. Ivar Gunn's account of the event is reprinted in *Irregular Memories of the 'Thirties*. Three annual dinners were held, but then personal complications, and Hitler, intervened. There was no dinner in 1937, and in March 1938 members received a postcard stating: 'The Sherlock Holmes Society – like the Red-Headed League – is dissolved.'

But England withstood the blasts of the east wind, and post-war recovery included plans for a 'Festival of Britain', to be held in 1951, the centenary of the Great Exhibition at Crystal Palace. Rationing was still in place, bombsites were much in evidence. The festival was intended as 'a tonic to the nation'.

The journalist James Edward Holroyd, while carrying out research at Marylebone Library, got into conversation with the assistant reference librarian, C.T. (Jack) Thorne. Wouldn't it be a good idea, they thought, to have a Sherlock Holmes exhibition as part of the festival? The borough council's preference was for an instructive exhibit on slum clearance, but when *The Times* began publishing letters of protest, from, among others, Dr Watson, Mycroft Holmes, Mrs Hudson and the famous actor Arthur Wontner, the councillors decided that Sherlock Holmes would be rather a good topic after all.

The exhibition was mounted in Abbey House, home of the Abbey National Building Society, whose address encompassed the magic number, 221 Baker Street. Fifty years on, Anthony Howlett remembered: 'The organiser and guiding spirit was Jack Thorne, and his helper was Freda Pearce, assistant librarian. At that time, I was a newly-fledged barrister with too much spare time on my hands, so I haunted that exhibition to lend what help I could.' He added: 'One striking fact about this project was the enthusiasm it created, and offers of help had poured in from members of the old Sherlock Holmes Society, from America and across the world, and from UK enthusiasts – many with invaluable specialist knowledge of Holmesiana. One such was Professor (then Doctor) W.T. Williams, who was responsible for the scientific exhibits.' Another volunteer was a young solicitor, Colin Prestige. Items for display came from many sources, including the families of Arthur Conan Doyle, Joseph Bell and Sidney Paget, whose daughter Winifred provided some of his original artwork. The centrepiece was the recreation of the sitting room of 221B, to the plans of the eminent theatre designer Michael Weight. The exhibition was a roaring success. In 1952 it moved on to New York, and eventually exhibits from it formed the displays at The Sherlock Holmes pub in London.

While they were still assembling the exhibition, Tony Howlett, Bill Williams, Jack Thorne, Freda Pearce and Colin Prestige decided that the time had come to resurrect The Sherlock Holmes Society – but, to indicate a rebirth, they chose the name The Sherlock Holmes Society of London. The first meeting was held on 18 April 1951 at Marylebone Library. Besides the founders, those present included Guy Warrack, author of *Sherlock Holmes and Music*; Winifred Paget; James Edward Holroyd; Michael Weight; Ian M. Leslie, author of Dr Watson's letter to *The Times*; and Sir Gerald Kelly, then president of the Royal Academy.

The first general meeting was held on 17 July 1951 at the Victoria and Albert Museum, when S.C. Roberts became the first president. *The Sherlock Holmes Journal* began publication in 1952, and Freda Pearce and Tony Howlett were married that same year. She succeeded him as president in 2003.

More than sixty years on the society continues to flourish, with nearly 1,200 full members and more than 200 associate members.

The year begins with the Annual Dinner, always an especially popular event. Over the decades guest speakers have included commissioners of the Metropolitan Police and the City of London Police; crime writers P.D. James, Michael Gilbert, H.R.F. Keating, Colin Dexter, Ruth Rendell, June Thomson and Simon Brett; actors Arthur Wontner, Carleton Hobbs, Douglas Wilmer and Mark Gatiss; Michael Cox, creator of Granada Television's *Sherlock Holmes* series, and Steven Moffat, co-creator of BBC Television's *Sherlock*; and all-rounders Benny Green, Barry Took, Barry Cryer, Stephen

Fry, Gyles Brandreth and Sandi Toksvig. Agatha Christie was a unique guest of honour in 1962: she accepted on the condition that she should not be required to make a speech!

Other events throughout the year may include talks, discussions, theatrical entertainments, a film evening, an annual lecture, a Victorian cricket match against the P.G. Wodehouse Society, and excursions around London and the UK to investigate the locations of the stories. The society has also ventured overseas, making six pilgrimages to Switzerland, with a seventh arranged for 2012. The final destination, of course, is the Reichenbach Falls, and each participant is required to represent a specific character from the stories and to wear appropriate Victorian costume.

Members of the Sherlock Holmes Society of London pause at an appropriate spot during the 2011 expedition to Oxford. *Photo copyright Jean Upton*

The society was closely involved with the commissioning and design of John Doubleday's statue of Sherlock Holmes at Meiringen in Switzerland in 1988, and was a sponsor, with the late Dame Jean Conan Doyle, of the Sherlock Holmes Museum in Meiringen, opened in 1991. The Sherlock Holmes Statue Company, responsible for the statue at Baker Street station in London, was set up for this purpose by the society.

Anyone with an interest in Sherlock Holmes is welcome to join. *The Sherlock Holmes Journal* is published twice a year, and a newsletter, *The District Messenger*, is published throughout the year and is available by email. Details are available on the website www.sherlock-holmes.org.uk

The Sherlock Holmes Journal published supplements in 2001 and 2011 that provide more detailed information on the origins of the society.

• OTHER SOCIETIES •

THE SCION SOCIETIES

The BSI meets formally only once a year at its annual dinner. However, there are satellite groups all over the United States – in fact, all over the world – known as scion societies. These meet throughout the year, produce their own newsletters or journals, and many have their own lapel badges, which are highly collectible. Peter Blau, secretary of the Baker Street Irregulars, maintains a list of Sherlockian societies throughout the world, which is accessible via Willis Frick's invaluable Sherlocktron website at http://sherlocktron.hostoi.com/Sherlocktron.html.

ORGANISATIONS IN THE UK

Since most of the Sherlock Holmes Society of London's activities are based in or near London, groups within the UK have formed to enable more localised meetings for its members. Those we know to be currently active are:

- The Scandalous Bohemians (the North of England)
- The Musgraves (formerly The Northern Musgraves)
- The Poor Folk upon the Moors (the Sherlock Holmes Society of the South West of England)
- The Crew of the SS Mayday ('Moored at Belfast')
- The Deerstalkers of Welshpool
- The Self-Important Scotland Yarders (The Sherlock Holmes Society of Scotland)
- The Sherlock Holmes Society of Cheltenham
- The Friends of Dr Watson (a special interest group rather than a regional group)

Contact information is available at http://sherlocktron.hostoi.com/Sherlocktron.html.

ORGANISATIONS AROUND THE WORLD

There are, of course, Sherlock Holmes societies throughout the world, in Australia, Belgium, Brazil, Canada, China, the Czech Republic, Denmark, France, Germany, India, Iran, Israel, Italy, Japan, Kyrgyzstan, Malaysia, New Zealand, Portugal, Russia, Spain, Sweden, and Switzerland, besides the UK and the USA. And there are some that really have no geographical base: the virtual societies, such as The Hounds of the Internet, which could only have existed within the past twenty years or so. The following are among the most senior groups:

THE BOOTMAKERS OF TORONTO

Canada's leading society was inspired by *A Weekend with Sherlock Holmes*, a conference held at the Metro Toronto Central Library in December 1971. At the first meeting, in February 1972, the name 'The Bootmakers of Toronto' was chosen because the boot stolen from Sir Henry Baskerville was made by 'Meyers, Toronto'; the elected president of the Bootmakers is given the title of 'Meyers'. Most of the meetings are held at the Toronto Reference Library, which owns one of the world's most important collections of material relating to Arthur Conan Doyle and his work, and the annual Blue Carbuncle Dinner is held at the Badminton and Racquet Club of Toronto. The Bootmakers also organise occasional international conferences, such as the 2011 'SinS' (A Study in Scandal), in partnership with the Friends of the Arthur Conan Doyle Collection.

In their quarterly journal *Canadian Holmes*, as at their meetings, the Bootmakers have always shown an admirable willingness to regard Holmes and Watson both as real people and as the fictional creations of Arthur Conan Doyle. Notable Bootmakers have included Cameron Hollyer, Hartley Nathan, Donald Redmond, Christopher Redmond, David Skene-Melvin, Maureen Green and Doug Wrigglesworth.

The Bootmakers's website is at www.sherlockian.net/bootmakers/index.html.

THE DANISH BAKER STREET IRREGULARS

There's a long tradition of Holmesian scholarship in Scandinavia. The Danish Baker Street Irregulars – otherwise the Sherlock Holmes Klubben i Danmark – was founded in 1950 by A.D. Henriksen. Besides the annual meeting and an excellent newsletter, *Sherlockiana*, the society sponsors two horse races each year at Aalborg: the Silver Blaze Sweepstakes and the Professor Moriarty Memorial. The Danish Irregulars's publications are notable for their erudition and their humour. It seems natural that the society's president in the 1970s was the charming, witty cartoonist and illustrator Henry Lauritzen.

The website is www.sherlockiana.dk/shklub/index_en.html.

THE SHERLOCK HOLMES SOCIETY OF FRANCE

Founded in 1993 by a group that included a leading journalist, Thierry Saint-Joanis, and a brilliant political cartoonist,

Jean-Pierre Cagnat, La Société Sherlock Holmes de France (also called Les Quincaillers de la Franco-Midland) quickly established a reputation as one of the most active and imaginative groups of its kind in the world. You can add friendly, flamboyant and artistic as well. The journal and newsletters are gloriously Victorian in style. Holmes's grandmother was French, and there are many other references to France in the stories. The society makes the most of them.

The website is www.sshf.com.

THE JAPAN SHERLOCK HOLMES CLUB

The period 1868 to 1912 was the Meiji era in Japan, when the country was opened up to Europeans, and many Japanese are interested in British culture of the period. Their interest also covers Sherlock Holmes, whose adventures were published there as early as 1894. The Japan Sherlock Holmes Club, founded in 1977 by Akane Higashiyama and the late Tsukasa Kobayashi, was not the first in the country, but it has long been the biggest, with over 1,000 members and at least a dozen subsidiary groups. The quality and quantity of learned papers published by the club and its scions is remarkably high. Besides the founders, internationally important members have included Kiyoshi Tanaka, Masamichi Higurashi and Hiroshi Takata.

In 1988 the club was responsible for the commissioning and erecting a statue of Sherlock Holmes, as a memorial to the translator Ken Nobuhara, at Karuizawa Town.

The website is at www.holmesjapan.jp/english/index.htm#titles.

THE SYDNEY PASSENGERS

There is only one reference in the Sherlock Holmes stories to the capital of New South Wales, so when this society was founded in 1985 the name was taken from 'The Adventure of the *Gloria Scott*'. Meetings, held about six times a year, are usually based on one of the stories, with a talk, a quiz, and sometimes a dramatised scene from the story. The society's journal, *The Passengers' Log*, is wonderfully stylish, thanks to the excellent illustrations and cartoons of Philip Cornell, and the standard of scholarship is high. Regular contributors include Bill Barnes, Kerry Murphy, Chris Sequeira and Rosane McNamara.

The website is at www.sherlock.on.net.

· 16 ·

'A FRAUDULENT
IMITATION, WATSON'

• ACCOUNTS FROM OTHER HANDS •

ARTHUR CONAN DOYLE'S SIXTY stories of Sherlock Holmes
are vastly outnumbered by the ones written by other people.
The process really began after 'The Final Problem' (in the
December 1893 issue of *The Strand Magazine*) told the world
that the sage of Baker Street was dead. In the public mind,
Holmes and his accessories – deerstalker hat, pipe, magnifying lens, violin – encapsulated the ideal of the detective. The
image was already an icon.

PASTICHE

Defined by the *Oxford English Dictionary* as a 'literary or other
work of art composed in the style of a known author', pastiche is usually taken, in the world of Sherlock Holmes, to
indicate affectionate and sincere imitation of Conan Doyle's
original, but things are rarely that straightforward.

The French author Maurice Leblanc appropriated Holmes as the only detective worthy to challenge the famous *gentleman cambrioleur* Arsène Lupin, but Conan Doyle understandably took exception, and the name was changed to 'Herlock Sholmès' – or in some English editions 'Holmlock Shears'. On a lower literary level, Sherlock Holmes quickly became a hero in the European pulp magazines, where he was given a young assistant named Harry Taxon in place of Dr Watson. From 1907 innumerable stories appeared on the bookstalls in Germany, France, Denmark, Spain, Poland, and even Croatia. Russia developed its own more intelligent and better written series.

In English-speaking countries, use of the character mostly took the form of humour or satire, a tradition that remains vigorous. Serious attempts to continue the Holmes chronicles came to the fore in 1944, with Ellery Queen's anthology *The Misadventures of Sherlock Holmes*, which included a few such – most famously 'The Adventure of the Unique *Hamlet*' by Vincent Starrett – among the mostly comic stories the editors had gathered from various sources. The book was short lived. Arthur Conan Doyle's sons detested the tongue-in-cheek 'scholarship' of the Sherlock Holmes societies, and jealously guarded their legal rights in his characters. After two printings *The Misadventures of Sherlock Holmes* was withdrawn from circulation.

Then the biographer Hesketh Pearson discovered the typescript of an unpublished Sherlock Holmes story among Conan Doyle's papers. In 1948 'The Case of the Man Who Was Wanted' was published in *Cosmopolitan*, but upon its British publication the following January the Conan Doyles received a letter from a retired architect named Arthur Whitaker, who

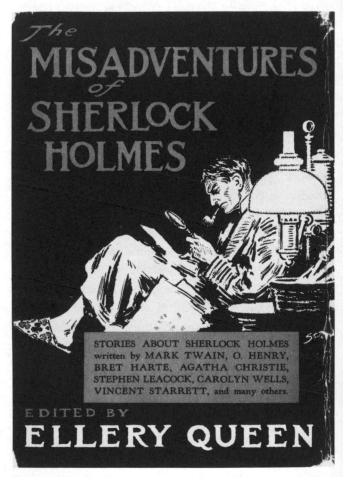

The Misadventures of Sherlock Holmes. The first important collection of pastiche and parody. *Collection of Roger Johnson and Jean Upton*

claimed that he had written the story in 1910 and sent it to Sir Arthur, who had given him ten guineas for the rights to the plot. Despite the family's angry denials, Whitaker proved his claim. 'The Case of the Man Who Was Wanted' is actually a pretty good story, in a fair imitation of Conan Doyle's style.

Ironically, the major contribution to Sherlock Holmes pastiche came in the early 1950s with a series of twelve stories by Adrian Conan Doyle himself, six of them written in collaboration with John Dickson Carr. They appeared in book form in 1954 as *The Exploits of Sherlock Holmes.* Despite the dismissive comment of Edgar W. Smith, head of the Baker Street Irregulars, that they should be called 'Sherlock Holmes Exploited', they are about as close to the real thing as any writer has got.

The first new Holmes long story appeared as late as 1966, and it is something of an oddity. *A Study in Terror* by Ellery Queen was based, without acknowledgement, on the script of the 1965 movie. In fact, the greater part of the book, the Holmesian pastiche, was the work of Paul W. Fairman, and it is competently written, though with its share of Americanisms and anachronisms. There have been other surprisingly good novels based on film and television, such as *Murder by Decree* by Robert Weverka, but the best of them is Michael & Mollie Hardwick's witty treatment of Billy Wilder & I.A.L. Diamond's witty script for *The Private Life of Sherlock Holmes.*

Besides *A Study in Terror* and *Murder by Decree* other books have been based on the premise that Holmes was engaged in the search for Jack the Ripper. *The Last Sherlock Holmes Story* by Michael Dibdin has a particularly nasty twist, and Kingsley Amis, who reviewed it, said that he hoped it really *was* the last Sherlock Holmes story. The best use of the theme is *Dust and Shadow* by Lyndsay Faye, which combines factual accuracy and fidelity to Conan Doyle in a truly gripping story.

The first wholly original Sherlock Holmes novel to be written by an author other than Arthur Conan Doyle was *The Seven-per-Cent Solution*, in which Nicholas Meyer adroitly reworked the story of Holmes's use of drugs and of his conflict with Professor Moriarty. It also set the fashion for having Holmes encounter celebrities, both from life and from literature; a fashion that Nicholas Meyer followed in his later Holmes novels, *The West End Horror* and *The Canary Trainer*. The unprecedented success of *The Seven-per-Cent Solution* encouraged other writers to try their hand; the encouragement has been further enhanced since by the final expiry of copyright (except in the USA) and the development of electronic publishing. The results have been mixed, to say the least.

The number of new Sherlock Holmes stories is already vast, and it's constantly growing. We can only mention some of the more interesting ones here.

Among the novels, those of the Canadian author L.B. Greenwood stand out. In *Sherlock Holmes and the Case of the Raleigh Legacy*, *The Case of Sabina Hall* and *The Case of the Thistle of Scotland* she captures style, character and atmosphere superbly. Barrie Roberts shows the same virtues in his nine books, beginning with *Sherlock Holmes and the Railway Maniac*. Few others have reached that standard.

The detective has also been placed in the thick of real-life events. *Sherlock Holmes and the Wood Green Empire Mystery* by W. Lane brings Holmes out of retirement to investigate the strange death of the magician Chung Ling Soo. More recently Donald Thomas has applied Holmes's methods, and Holmes himself, to real-life mysteries, in a series of books that began with *The Secret Cases of Sherlock Holmes*.

The Seven-per-Cent Solution inspired many more tales in which the detective encounters real-life celebrities in fictional circumstances. In *The Adventure of the Stalwart Companions* by H. Paul Jeffers, he and Theodore Roosevelt investigate a murder in New York. Daniel Stashower, Lee A. Matthias, and P.H. Cannon are just three of the authors who have teamed Holmes with Harry Houdini. He has also had dealings with Oscar Wilde in novels by Russell Brown and Milo Yelesiyevich.

Some have matched Holmes with characters created by other authors. Holmes, Watson and Professor Challenger faced H.G. Wells's Martian invaders in *Sherlock Holmes' War of the Worlds* by Manly Wade Wellman and Wade Wellman. The title of *Sherlock Holmes vs Dracula* by Loren D. Estleman is self-explanatory. A good later variant of the theme is *The Tangled Skein* by David Stuart Davies. Sherlock Holmes and Dr Fu Manchu are antagonists in *Ten Years Beyond Baker Street* by Cay Van Ash.

In *Exit Sherlock Holmes* by Robert Lee Hall, Holmes and Moriarty are visitors from the far distant future. Many science-fiction writers have been attracted to the characters of Holmes and Watson, and there have been at least three important anthologies – *Sherlock Holmes through Time and*

Space, *Sherlock Holmes in Orbit* and *The Improbable Adventures of Sherlock Holmes* — as well as various novels and innumerable comic books and graphic novels. The detective has also faced supernatural threats despite his statement that 'No ghosts need apply'. Collections include *Ghosts in Baker Street*, *Shadows over Baker Street* and *Gaslight Grimoire*.

⁕⁓◦⦊⦉◦⁓⁕

Replicating Conan Doyle's style is harder than it seems, and some authors have avoided the trap by not using Dr Watson as the narrator. Sidney Silchester, who recounts the events of *A Taste for Honey* by H.F. Heard, is so different from Watson that he has never even heard of the great detective! Lloyd Biggle Jr introduced a former irregular, Porter Jones, as the detective's 'leg-man' and narrator in *The Quallsford Inheritance* and *The Glendower Conspiracy*. Laurie R. King achieved outstanding and continuing success with her novels about Mary Russell — who became Holmes's wife. The series, which began with *The Beekeeper's Apprentice*, has attracted devotees worldwide. The same is true of Carole Nelson Douglas's novels about Irene Adler, the first being *Good Night, Mr Holmes*.

Some authors have used one of Holmes's associates as the central character. The first important work of this kind is probably *The Return of Moriarty* by John Gardner, published in 1974, which convincingly portrays the Napoleon of crime as a sort of Victorian Don Corleone. There have been two sequels. Professor Moriarty takes centre stage in other stories too, such as Michael Kurland's *The Infernal Device*. Sherlock's brother Mycroft Holmes is the protagonist of *Enter the Lion* by

Michael P. Hodel and Sean M. Wright, and of at least two different series of novels, by Glen Petrie and by Quinn Fawcett, with a third just starting. This, beginning with *Mycroft Holmes and the Adventure of the Silver Birches*, is the work of David Dickinson. In *The Adventures of Inspector Lestrade* and its sequels, by M. J. Trow, Sholto Lestrade is a put-upon but ultimately triumphant hero, and Sherlock Holmes a pompous fraud. These are both ingenious detective stories and very funny comedies.

A recent novel, *Barefoot on Baker Street* by Charlotte Anne Walters, tells the powerful story of an orphan girl who survives poverty and violence to become a vital part of life for Holmes and Watson. Traditionalists may prefer *The House of Silk* by Anthony Horowitz.

The essence of Sherlock Holmes is in the short stories however, and it is the short pastiches that have most often succeeded in recreating the true Holmes.

The two best series are the work, respectively, of Denis O. Smith and June Thomson. The former's four volumes of *The Chronicles of Sherlock Holmes* are not easy to find, though it's likely that they will be issued as e-books. The latter has followed Adrian Conan Doyle & John Dickson Carr in presenting the truth behind some of Dr Watson's hints. *The Secret Files of Sherlock Holmes*, published in 1990, has been followed by four more, with another due in 2012. Both authors capture the style and substance of the original with remarkable accuracy.

Besides *The Misadventures of Sherlock Holmes*, there are two exceptional anthologies of Holmesian pastiche. Richard

Lancelyn Green reprinted eleven stories in *The Further Adventures of Sherlock Holmes*, all of very high quality, and for *The Mammoth Book of New Sherlock Holmes Adventures* Mike Ashley devised his own chronology of the detective's career, and arranged the twenty-six new adventures to fit.

PARODY

'My Evening with Sherlock Holmes' was published anonymously as early as 1891, just four months after the first of the adventures appeared in *The Strand Magazine*. In 2011 Charles Press established that the author was in fact Arthur Conan Doyle's friend J.M. Barrie. It was the first of an apparently infinite number of parodies, spoofs and jokes. We shall recommend just three remarkable collections.

⤙◦❦◦⤚

In 1893 'The Bishop's Crime' initiated *The Adventures of Picklock Holes* by 'Cunnin' Toil': actually R.C. Lehmann, who devised ingenious parallel plots for each story. As Tom and Enid Schantz observed in the introduction to their 1974 reprint of the first series: 'there is always a perfectly innocent situation and a far more sinister one invented by Holes.' His success is achieved, in fact, 'by planting the evidence or, in extreme cases, by hiring the criminal'!

When Frank Richards created Greyfriars School, Harry Wharton and Billy Bunter he also created *The Greyfriars Herald*, where, in 1915, Herlock Sholmes made his début. His farcical misadventures were chronicled at frequent intervals over the

The Memoirs of Schlock Homes. The second volume of Robert L. Fish's brilliant spoofs. *Collection of Roger Johnson and Jean Upton*

next ten years, and he even made a couple of appearances as late as the 1950s. The stories are mostly broad and funny burlesques, but they can be subtle, and sometimes uncomfortably pointed. Ninety-five were collected in *The Complete Casebook of Herlock Sholmes* – not quite all, but nearly.

Finally there is Schlock Homes. Between 1960 and 1981 Robert L. Fish contributed thirty-two deliriously funny adventures of Schlock Homes of Bagel Street, as narrated by his friend Dr Watney. Fish was a brilliant punster, but the real delight is the inspired double plotting of each story. Homes is an innocent with a genius for misapplied logic, and as Tom and Enid Schantz noted: 'There are always two crimes in a Schlock Homes story, the real crime and the one Schlock solves.' The contents of *Schlock Homes: The Complete Bagel Street Saga* are deeply satisfying.

17

'MAYBE YOU COLLECT YOURSELF, SIR'

• COLLECTING SHERLOCK HOLMES •

TWENTY YEARS AGO, WHEN we were preparing to move house, the removal men came around to give us an estimate. After their initial reaction of disbelief and stifled guffaws, they stated that the only time they had moved so many books was when they helped to relocate a bookshop in a neighbouring town. The study, where much of our collection is now housed, is sometimes called the 'Omigod' room, for obvious reasons.

Ours is hardly the largest private collection, but it isn't untypical of a Sherlockian household, with a wide-ranging mélange of canonical books and objects. How a nineteenth-century detective could spawn such an overwhelming variety of merchandise never ceases to amaze even long-time, hard-core collectors.

Some collectors are quite specific as to their preferred areas of interest. We know of several who collect only first editions, and another who concentrates on foreign language translations. One collects only *The Hound of the Baskervilles* in all of its various editions. Then there are completists, whose floorboards creak ominously under the strain of bookshelves stuffed with every conceivable publication containing even the most casual and obscure mention of Sherlock Holmes.

Three-dimensional curios come in sufficient quantity and variety to suit any interest, budget or taste, however question-able the latter might be. There are top-of-the-range bronze sculptures, the collectible Royal Doulton figures and charac-ter jugs, and maquettes of public statues of Sherlock Holmes. There are also pewter figures of Holmes, Watson and others, such as the excellent ones by Charles Hall of Edinburgh. Animal lovers can choose from countless anthropomorphic versions of Holmes and Watson. Within our own collection alone they are depicted as a cat, dog, pig, owl, hedgehog, dragon, rabbit, fox, mouse, frog and bear. We would not be surprised to learn of the existence of deerstalkered wombats.

Arctophiles can take their pick of teddy bears in all shapes, sizes and materials. There are small moulded resin figurines, beanbag teddies, inexpensive commercially produced soft toys, high-quality limited editions, and hand-crafted spe-cially commissioned bears. One of our favourites is Bearlock Holmes, a substantially chunky fellow who will considerately share a chair with our cats when they are feeling sociable. Another is a delightful little chap, about 7in tall, made for us by a very talented friend.

Many cartoon characters have been depicted as Holmes in miniatures, soft toys, books, jigsaw puzzles and games

Collectibles. *Photo copyright Jean Upton*

Snoopy, the Pink Panther, Mickey Mouse, Sherlock Hemlock from Sesame Street, Scooby Doo, Angelica from Rugrats, and, of course, Basil of Baker Street.

For philatelists there are Holmesian stamps from Switzerland, San Marino, Nicaragua, the Turks & Caicos Islands, Dominica, Guernsey and East Timor, as well as the United Kingdom. Numismatists can choose from handsome coins from Gibraltar and the Cook Islands.

Want to spice up your wardrobe? There are t-shirts, sweatshirts, neckties, bowties, scarves, wristwatches, pocket watches, lapel pins and fine jewellery. To make a really serious impression, you can even get a custom-made Inverness cloak and deerstalker. That handsome Belstaff overcoat Benedict

Cumberbatch wears may be beyond your reach, but there are tailors in the Far East who make copies at a tenth of the price. And we have an uneasy suspicion that someone, somewhere, is selling Sherlock Holmes underpants.

If you must fill every waking moment of every day with reminders of the Great Detective, there are teapots, mugs, coasters, clothes brushes, letter racks, thimbles, walking sticks, letter openers, key rings, tea towels, aprons, pipes, rubber stamps, clocks, Christmas ornaments, mousemats, cigars, wall plaques, chocolates, fridge magnets and book-marks. You name it, there's a deerstalker on it.

One of us collects the autographs of actors who have played Holmes or Watson (the other one is gratifyingly tolerant). As we have discovered, most actors like to know that their work is appreciated, and they are happy to oblige if you ask politely. An invaluable tool here is the *Spotlight Directory* at www.spotlight.com, where a performer's entry will give contact details for his or her agent.

THE MAJOR COLLECTIONS

The great Sherlockian collectors are often extraordinarily generous. John Bennett Shaw, the much loved and greatly missed 'Sage of Santa Fe', cheerfully admitted to having 'the selectivity of a vacuum-cleaner' when it came to amassing Sherlockiana. A huge number of books and artefacts shared space with such mind-bending curve balls as the Professor Moriarty toilet seat, deerstalkered chocolate rabbits in the freezer and some hor-rifyingly naff nylon underpants imprinted with a strategically placed magnifying lens. John's BSI investiture was 'The Hans Sloane of My Age', after the man whose collection formed the foundation of the British Museum.

If John had a duplicate, he would pass it on. In turn, friends who came across something new or bizarre would send it to him, and receive in reply a grateful note saying 'You are a benefactor of the race', quoting Watson's to Holmes at the end of 'The Red-Headed League'.

Late in his life, John wanted to ensure that others would have access to his accumulated treasures. Every item, warts and all, was carefully catalogued, packed up and dispatched to the University of Minnesota, whose collection of Sherlockiana was founded in 1974 when it bought James C. Iraldi's library of first editions. John Shaw's bequest made the university's Sherlock Holmes Collection the largest and most diverse in the world. John died in 1994 followed by his wife Dorothy in 1999, but their memory and friendship lives on in the Sherlock Holmes Collection.

University of Minnesota, Twin Cities Campus,
Minneapolis, Minnesota.
http://special.lib.umn.edu/rare/holmes.phtml

⁂

Richard Lancelyn Green (1954–2004) began collecting as a small child, using his pocket money to pick up interesting little odds and ends, and eventually created his own full-scale version of the 221B sitting room in the attic of his family home at Poulton Hall near Liverpool. Perhaps unsurprisingly, Richard's parents, Roger and June, were long-time members of the Sherlock Holmes Society of London. For more than forty years Richard sought and obtained both Holmesiana and Doyleana. On many occasions we've asked whether a book-seller or vendor had anything related to Holmes or Conan Doyle, and been told: 'We always set those items aside for a special client.' Once the seller realised that we understood the situation ('It's Richard, isn't it?') he'd relax, and would sometimes come up with a duplicate of an item that he knew Richard already had.

Over the years Richard managed to lay his hands on the crown jewels of Sherlockiana, including original artwork by Sidney Paget, a pipe belonging to the actor H.A. Saintsbury and Conan Doyle's own writing desk. If you imagined what you would most like to have in your own collection, you could bet that Richard had it. He had been gathering material for a definitive biography of Arthur Conan Doyle, and was deeply dis-mayed when a cache of material that he'd thought earmarked for the British Library was sent to auction at Christie's in London. Richard's untimely death occurred just two months before the sale took place, inspiring the media to whip up nonsensical rumours about purported cloak-and-dagger conspiracies and a conveniently manufactured 'curse of Conan Doyle'.

Eccentric but practical, Richard had already bequeathed his collection to the City of Portsmouth. With the aid of his family and knowledgeable friends, it took two weeks to pack and was estimated to consist of over 200,000 items. In early 2012 the process of cataloguing continues. A Conan Doyle Archive Research Centre was opened within Portsmouth Central Library in 2011, and scholars are already taking advantage of

Catherine Cooke with a few of the treasures at the Sherlock Holmes Collection at Marylebone Library. *Photo copyright Jean Upton*

the documentary materials, including unique photographs and ephemera. At the City Museum an impressive exhibition entitled 'A Study in Sherlock' comprises a quite remarkable selection of items, plus interactive displays and a narration by the collection's patron, Stephen Fry.

We still talk of Richard with affection and miss him very much. When the Sherlock Holmes Society of London made its pilgrimage to Switzerland in 2005, a special service on an Alpine mountainside was held in memory of Richard, who had served as chairman of the society from 1996 to 1999.

Portsmouth Library Service, Portsmouth, England
www.conandoylecollection.co.uk

At the heart of Marylebone Library's Sherlock Holmes Collection is a bookcase donated by the Sherlock Holmes Society of London in 1959 to mark Sir Arthur Conan Doyle's centenary. For the past thirty years the curator and guardian has been Catherine Cooke, who, like her predecessor Heather Owen, is a leading member of the Sherlock Holmes Society of London. The collection is modest by comparison with some others, but it contains a great deal that the researcher will need, and it is only a matter of yards from Baker Street itself. Access to the collection is by appointment only.

Marylebone Library, Westminster, England
www.westminster.gov.uk/services/libraries/special/sherlock

The major resource for students of Holmes's creator is the Arthur Conan Doyle collection in Toronto. It was begun in 1969 when librarian Cameron Hollyer persuaded the city to purchase 150 volumes from the library of Arthur Baillie and a lot of 1,500 items from Harold Mortlake. The following year a large archive of ephemera from Judge S. Tupper Bigelow was added, and since then the collection has grown through purchases and donations and now includes some very rare and desirable material, including the manuscript of Conan Doyle's play *Angels of Darkness*. Unpublished until 2001, the play is loosely based on the American episode of 'A Study in Scarlet'; it features Dr Watson but not Sherlock Holmes.

Toronto Public Library, Toronto, Ontario
www.torontopubliclibrary.ca/books-video-music/specialized-collections/literature-genre-doyle.jsp

The Baker Street Irregulars Trust Archive, housed in the Houghton Library at Harvard University, is unusually specialised, as it consists solely of the large and ever increasing collection of material relating to the senior American Holmes society. As the website notes, in 2003, Michael Whelan, 'Wiggins' of The Baker Street Irregulars, decided that the BSI's archive of correspondence, photographic and audio materials, manuscripts of historical documents, biographical material, newspaper clippings, and magazine articles regarding the history of the BSI and individual Irregulars should be properly housed and accessible for research. The archive was formally opened in November 2005.

Harvard University. Houghton Library, Cambridge, Massachusetts
http://oasis.lib.harvard.edu/oasis/deliver/deepLink?_collection=o
asis&uniqueId=hou02178
www.bsitrust.org/archive

<hr />

In the United Kingdom, other notable collections are held at the British Library in London, the National Library of Scotland in Edinburgh, and the Royal College of Surgeons of Edinburgh.

An unexpected delight is the Conan Doyle Collection at the Bibliothèque Cantonale et Universitaire at Lausanne, Switzerland.

In the United States there are collections at the Athenaeum of Philadelphia in Philadelphia, Pennsylvania; Birmingham Southern College, Birmingham, Alabama; Huntington Library, San Marino, California; the Lilly Library at Indiana

University, Bloomington, Indiana; New York Public Library; the Newberry Library in Chicago; University of Michigan at Ann Arbor; University of North Carolina, Chapel Hill; The Harry Ransom Humanities Research Center at the University of Texas, Austin; and the University of Tulsa, Oklahoma.

Fuller information about these holdings can be found on the website of the Sub-Librarians' Scion of the Baker Street Irregulars at http://elisanonline.com/sublibrarians/libraries.html.

18

'WE KNOW THE CODE'

In 1947 Professor Jay Finley Christ devised four-letter abbreviations for the titles of the sixty stories. Generally speaking, they should be used sparingly!

ABBE	The Abbey Grange
BERY	The Beryl Coronet
BLAC	Black Peter
BLAN	The Blanched Soldier
BLUE	The Blue Carbuncle
BOSC	The Boscombe Valley Mystery
BRUC	The Bruce-Partington Plans
CARD	The Cardboard Box
CHAS	Charles Augustus Milverton
COPP	The Copper Beeches
CREE	The Creeping Man
CROO	The Crooked Man
DANC	The Dancing Men
DEVI	The Devil's Foot
DYIN	The Dying Detective

EMPT	The Empty House
ENGR	The Engineer's Thumb
FINA	The Final Problem
FIVE	The Five Orange Pips
GLOR	The Gloria Scott
GOLD	The Golden Pince-nez
GREE	The Greek Interpreter
HOUN	The Hound of the Baskervilles
IDEN	A Case of Identity
ILLU	The Illustrious Client
LADY	The Disappearance of Lady Frances Carfax
LAST	His Last Bow
LION	The Lion's Mane
MAZA	The Mazarin Stone
MISS	The Missing Three-Quarter
MUSG	The Musgrave Ritual
NAVA	The Naval Treaty
NOBL	The Noble Bachelor
NORW	The Norwood Builder
PRIO	The Priory School
REDC	The Red Circle
REDH	The Red-Headed League
REIG	The Reigate Squires
RESI	The Resident Patient
RETI	The Retired Colourman
SCAN	A Scandal in Bohemia
SECO	The Second Stain
SHOS	Shoscombe Old Place
SIGN	The Sign of the Four

SILV	Silver Blaze
SIXN	The Six Napoleons
SOLI	The Solitary Cyclist
SPEC	The Speckled Band
STOC	The Stockbroker's Clerk
STUD	A Study in Scarlet
SUSS	The Sussex Vampire
THOR	The Problem of Thor Bridge
3GAB	The Three Gables
3GAR	The Three Garridebs
3STU	The Three Students
TWIS	The Man with the Twisted Lip
VALL	The Valley of Fear
VEIL	The Veiled Lodger
WIST	The Wisteria Lodge
YELL	The Yellow Face

· BIBLIOGRAPHY ·

'SEVERAL TRUSTWORTHY BOOKS OF REFERENCE'

· SOME RECOMMENDED READING ·

TENS OF THOUSANDS OF books have been written about Sherlock Holmes and his creator. Some are essential reading for anyone with more than a passing interest in the subject, while others, particularly in the fiction category, often make us wish that desktop publishing had never been invented. Separating the worthwhile from the worthless is a monumental task, whether one is a long-time collector or a novice.

John Bennett Shaw did aficionados and collectors an inestimable service by compiling what he called the Basic Holmesian Library, and over the years the 'Shaw 100' has been issued as a booklet by several different small publishers. The list is accessible on-line at http://webspace.webring.com/people/sp/porlock/ shaw_yop.html and on a couple of other websites. If you are interested in delving more deeply into the world of Sherlock Holmes, we urge you to investigate his recommendations.

Here we have categorised our own reference sources, along with other recommended reading, to help you to search further in your specific areas of interest. Our list includes titles from the Shaw 100, and some that were published after John Bennett Shaw's death in 1993.

Happily, many books that had been out of print have since been republished and several are now available electronically.

SIR ARTHUR CONAN DOYLE

Conan Doyle, Sir A., *Memories and Adventures* (Hodder and Stoughton, 1924)
Stashower, D., *Teller of Tales: The Life of Arthur Conan Doyle* (Allen Lane, The Penguin Press, 2000)
Lycett, A., *Conan Doyle: The Man Who Created Sherlock Holmes* (Weidenfeld & Nicolson, 2007)
Lellenberg, J., Stashower, D. and Foley, C. (eds), *Arthur Conan Doyle: A Life in Letters* (HarperPress, 2007)

THE ORIGINAL STORIES BY SIR ARTHUR CONAN DOYLE – 'THE CANON'

The most easily available text these days is the one originally published in 1930 by Doubleday, Doran of New York, which contains minor differences from what, until the 1980s, was the standard British version, published by John Murray and based on the original *Strand Magazine* texts (Captain Croker became Captain Crocker in America, for instance).

The canon has never been out of print, and it is unlikely that it ever will be. A quick browse around your local bookshop or on the internet will confirm that there are many attractive editions available, at prices ranging from the enticingly cheap to the jaw-droppingly expensive.

Conan Doyle, Sir A., edited and annotated by Leslie S. Klinger, *The New Annotated Sherlock Holmes*, 3 vols (W.W. Norton, 2004–5)

—, edited and annotated by Owen Dudley Edwards, Richard Lancelyn Green, Christopher Roden and W.W. Robson, *The Oxford Sherlock Holmes*, 9 vols (Oxford University Press, 1993)

—, edited and annotated by William S. Baring-Gould, *The Annotated Sherlock Holmes* (John Murray, 1968)

DRAMATISATIONS

Barnes, A., *Sherlock Holmes on Screen* (Titan Books, 2011)

Coules, B., *221BBC: Writing for the World's First Complete Dramatised Canon* (The Northern Musgraves, 1998)

Cox, M., *A Study in Celluloid: A Producer's Account of Jeremy Brett as Sherlock Holmes* (Gasogene Books, 2011)

— (ed.), *The Baker Street File: A Guide to the Appearance and Habits of Sherlock Holmes and Dr. Watson* (Calabash Press, 1997)

Davies, D.S., *Starring Sherlock Holmes* (Titan Books, 2007)

Field, A.J., *England's Secret Weapon: The Wartime Films of Sherlock Holmes* (Middlesex University Press, 2009)

Haining, P., *The Television Sherlock Holmes* (Virgin Books, 1994)

Hall, C. and Blythe, P., 'On Stage Sherlock Holmes: Comedy, Drama and Musicals', chapbook, 2 vols (Charles Hall, 1997)

Hoey, M.A., *Sherlock Holmes & the Fabulous Faces: The Universal Pictures Repertory Company* (Bearmanor Media, 2011)

Kabatchnik, A., *Sherlock Holmes on the Stage* (Scarecrow Press, 2008)

USEFUL REFERENCES

Bullard, S.R., and Collins, M.L., *Who's Who in Sherlock Holmes: A Complete and Handy Reference to the Great Detective's Every Case* (Taplinger Publishing Co., 1980)

Redmond, C., *Sherlock Holmes Handbook* (Dundurn Press, 2009)

Tracy, J., *The Encyclopaedia Sherlockiana* (Doubleday & Co., 1977)

SHERLOCKIAN SCHOLARSHIP (WRITINGS ABOUT THE WRITINGS)

Bayard, P., *Sherlock Holmes Was Wrong: Reopening the Case of The Hound of the Baskervilles* (Bloomsbury, 2008)

Bigelow, S.T., *The Baker Street Briefs* (Metropolitan Toronto Reference Library, 1993)

Blakeney, T.S., *Sherlock Holmes: Fact or Fiction?* (John Murray, 1932)

Campbell, M., *Sherlock Holmes* (Pocket Essentials, 2007)

Dahlinger, S.E., and Klinger, L.S. (eds), *Sherlock Holmes, Conan Doyle & The Bookman: Pastiches, Parodies, Letters, Columns and Commentary from America's 'Magazine of Literature and Life' (1895–1933)* (Gasogene Books, 2010)

Hall, T.H., *Sherlock Holmes: Ten Literary Studies* (Gerald Duckworth & Co., 1969)

—, *The Late Mr. Sherlock Holmes, and Other Literary Studies* (Gerald Duckworth & Co., 1971)

Harrison, M., *A Study in Surmise: The Making of Sherlock Holmes* (Gaslight Publications, 1984)

Holroyd, J.E., *Baker Street By-ways: A Book About Sherlock Holmes* (George Allen & Unwin, 1959)

Hyder, W., *From Baltimore to Baker Street: Thirteen Sherlockian Studies* (Metropolitan Toronto Reference Library, 1995)

King, L.R., and Klinger, L.S. (eds.), *The Grand Game: A Celebration of Sherlockian Scholarship, Volume One 1902–1959* (The Baker Street Irregulars, 2011)

—, *The Grand Game: A Celebration of Sherlockian Scholarship, Volume Two 1960–2010* (The Baker Street Irregulars, 2012)

McQueen, I., *Sherlock Holmes Detected: The Problems of the Long Stories* (David & Charles, 1974)

Morley, C., *Sherlock Holmes and Dr. Watson: A Textbook of Friendship* (Harcourt, Brace and Co., 1944)

Redmond, C. (ed.), *Canadian Holmes: The First Twenty-Five Years* (Calabash Press, 1997)

Redmond, D.A., *Sherlock Holmes: A Study in Sources* (McGill Queen's University Press, 1982)

Roberts, S.C., *Holmes and Watson: A Miscellany* (Oxford University Press, 1953)

Rothman, S. (ed.), *'A Remarkable Mixture': Award-Winning Articles from The Baker Street Journal* (The Baker Street Irregulars, 2007)

— (ed.), *The Standard Doyle Company: Christopher Morley on Sherlock Holmes*, (Fordham University Press, 1990)

Sauvage, L., with McKuras, J. and Vizoskie, S. (eds), *Sherlockian Heresies*, (Gasogene Books, 2010)

Shreffler, P.A. (ed.), *Sherlock Holmes by Gas-Lamp: Highlights from the First Four Decades of The Baker Street Journal* (Fordham University Press, 1989)

Smith, E.W. (ed.), *Profile by Gaslight: An Irregular Reader About the Private Life of Sherlock Holmes* (Simon & Schuster, 1944)

Starrett, V., compiled and annotated by Murdock, K., *Sherlock Alive: Sherlockian Excerpts from VS's 'Books Alive' Column in The Chicago Tribune 1942–1967* (The Battered Silicon Dispatch Box, 2010)

Utechin, N. (ed.), *The Best of The Sherlock Holmes Journal, Volume One* (The Sherlock Holmes Society of London, 2006)

—, *The Best of The Sherlock Holmes Journal, Volume Two* (The Sherlock Holmes Society of London, 2011)

ILLUSTRATED BOOKS

Blackbeard, B., *Sherlock Holmes in America* (Harry N. Abrams, 1981)

Hall, C., *The Sherlock Holmes Collection: The Great Detective and his Creator* (Charles Hall, 1987)

Eyles, A., *Sherlock Holmes, A Centenary Celebration* (John Murray, 1986)

Haining, P. (ed.), *The Sherlock Holmes Scrapbook* (New English Library, 1973)

Pointer, M., *The Pictorial History of Sherlock Holmes* (Bison Books for WH Smith, 1991)

BIOGRAPHICAL STUDIES OF SHERLOCK HOLMES AND DR WATSON

Brend, G., *My Dear Holmes: A Study in Sherlock* (George Allen & Unwin, 1951)

Carr, M., *In Search of Dr. Watson: A Sherlockian Investigation*, second, revised edition (MX Publishing, 2011)

Starrett, V., with Betzner, R. (ed.), *The Private Life of Sherlock Holmes – 75th Anniversary Edition* (Gasogene Books, 2008) N.B. Do not confuse this with the novelisation of the film with the same title, written by Michael and Mollie Hardwick.

Thomson, J., *Holmes and Watson: A Study in Friendship* (Constable, 1995)

'BIOGRAPHIES' OF SHERLOCK HOLMES AND DR WATSON

Baring-Gould, W.S., *Sherlock Holmes: A Biography of the World's First Consulting Detective* (Rupert Hart-Davis, 1962)

Hardwick, M., *Sherlock Holmes: My Life and Crimes* (Harvill Press, 1984)

—, *The Private Life of Dr. Watson: Being the Personal Reminiscences of John H. Watson, MD* (Weidenfeld & Nicolson, 1983)

Harrison, M., *I, Sherlock Holmes: Memoirs of Mr. Sherlock Holmes, OM, late Consulting Private Detective-in-Ordinary to Their Majesties Queen Victoria, King Edward VII and King George V* (E.P. Dutton, 1977)

Mitchelson, A., *The Baker Street Irregular: The Unauthorised Biography of Sherlock Holmes* (Ian Henry Publications, 1994)

Rennison, N., *Sherlock Holmes: The Unauthorized Biography* (Atlantic Books, 2005)

CHRONOLOGY – THE TIMELINE OF THE CANON

Bell, H.W., *Sherlock Holmes and Dr. Watson: The Chronology of Their Adventures* (Magico Magazine, 1984)

Christ, J.F., *An Irregular Chronology of Sherlock Holmes of Baker Street* (Magico Magazine, 1985)

Delay, V., *Holmes and Watson: A New Chronology of Their Adventures* (The Sherlock Holmes Society of London, 2008)

Hall, J., *'I Remember the Date Very Well': A Chronology of the Sherlock Holmes Stories of Arthur Conan Doyle* (Ian Henry Publications/Players Press, 1993)

Peck, A.J. and Klinger, L.S., *'The Date Being —?': A Compendium of Chronological Data* (Magico Magazine, 1996)

Weber, J.E., *Under the Darkling Sky: A Chrono-Geographic Odyssey through the Holmesian Canon* (The Battered Silicon Dispatch Box, 2010)

Zeisler, E.B., *Baker Street Chronology: Commentaries on The Sacred Writings of Dr. John H.Watson* (Magico Magazine, 1983)

TOPOGRAPHY – THE WORLD OF HOLMES AND WATSON

Alexander, A.M., *Hot On The Scent: A Visitor's Guide to the London of Sherlock Holmes* (Calabash Press, 1999)

Davies, B., *Holmes and Watson Country: Travels in Search of Solutions*, 2 vols (The Sherlock Holmes Society of London, 2008)

Duncan, A., *Close to Holmes: A Look at the Connections Between Historical London, Sherlock Holmes and Sir Arthur Conan Doyle* (MX Publishing, 2009)

Foster, A., *Sherlock Holmes and Conan Doyle Locations: A Visitor's Guide* (McFarland & Co., 2011)

Hammer, D.L., *The Game is Afoot: A Travel Guide to the England of Sherlock Holmes* (Gasogene Press, 1983)

—, *For the Sake of the Game: Being a Further Travel Guide to the England of Sherlock Holmes* (Gasogene Press, 1986)

—, *The Worth of the Game: Being a Final Travel Guide to the England of Sherlock Holmes* (Gasogene Press, 1993)

Harrison, M., *In the Footsteps of Sherlock Holmes*, revised edition (David & Charles, 1971)

—, *The London of Sherlock Holmes* (David & Charles, 1972)

Sinclair, D., *Sherlock Holmes's London* (Robert Hale, 2009)

Viney, C., *Sherlock Holmes in London: A Photographic Record of Conan Doyle's Stories* (Equation, 1989)

Weller, P., *The Hound of the Baskervilles: Hunting the Dartmoor Legend* (Devon Books, 2001)

Wheeler, T.B., *The London of Sherlock Holmes, with GPS Addresses and e-Book Hyperlinks to Google Map StreetViews* (MX Publishing, 2011)

Wolff M.D., J., *The Sherlockian Atlas* (Magico Magazine, 1984)

HANDBOOKS PRODUCED BY THE SHERLOCK HOLMES SOCIETY OF LONDON FOR THEIR VISITS TO VARIOUS CANONICAL SITES

Bird, M. (ed.), *Sail and Steam*, Norfolk (2000)

—, *An East Wind*, Suffolk and Essex (1997)

—, *A Study in Dark Blue: Sherlock Holmes and Oxford* (1988)

—, *In the Country of the Broads: An Investigation into 'The 'Gloria Scott' and 'The Dancing Men'*, Norfolk (1984)

Bruxner, P. (ed.), *Sunday in Sussex*, Sussex (1993)

—, *In Beds with Sherlock Holmes*, Bedfordshire (1994)

—, *Fetlocks, Femurs and Phalanges*, Berkshire (1995)

—, *Going for a Soldier*, Royal Military Academy Sandhurst (1996)

—, *A Gaggle of Governesses*, Surrey and Hampshire (1997)

—, *The Cornish Horror*, Cornwall (1998)

Bruxner, P. and Ellis, B. (eds), *Helping Out Hopeless Hopkins*, Kent and Sussex (2001)

— , *Sussex Revamped*, Sussex (2004)

— , *Colour It Prussian Blue*, South London and Essex (2005)

Davies, B., *A Ramble Through the Ragged Shaw, and Other Studies at the Priory School*, Derbyshire (1985)

Ellis, B. and Marriott, G. (eds), *Meet Me in Bohemia: A Sherlock Holmes Czech Book*, Prague (2007)

—, *I Proceeded to Portsmouth*, Portsmouth (2008)

Ellis, B. (ed.), *This Dark Square: A Priory School Examination*, Derbyshire (2006)

Green, R.L. (ed.), *Lend Me Your Ears*, Liverpool and New Brighton (2003)

Horrocks, P. and Green, R.L. (eds), The *Return of Sherlock Holmes: The Handbook of the Sherlock Holmes Statue Festival*, London (1999)

Horrocks, P. (ed.), *The Tri-Metallic Question*, Winchester (1991)

Johnson, R. and Upton, J. (eds), *Back to Baker Street: An Appreciation of Sherlock Holmes and London*, London (1994)

McCafferty, J. (ed.), *The Light Is Dark Enough*, Cambridge (1989)

—, *Surrey with a Fringe*, Surrey and Hampshire (2010)

Porter, P. and Cooke, C. (eds), *France in the Blood: A Practical Handbook of French Holmesian Culture, with Some Observations* (1993)

Purves, S. (ed.), *Hound and Horse: A Dartmoor Commonplace Book* (1992)

——, *Radical Rethinks on Hound and Horse*, Dartmoor (2002)

Smyth, A. (ed.), *The Boscombe Valley Mystery Tour: A Light Hearted Look at the West*, Herefordshire (1999)

FOOD AND DRINK

Guy, P., *Bacchus at Baker Street: Sherlock Holmes & Victorian Drinking Lore* (iUniverse, 2007)

Rosenblatt, J.C. and Sonnenschmidt, F.H., *Dining with Sherlock Holmes: A Baker Street Cookbook* (Thames & Hudson, 1978)

THE ADVENTURESSES OF SHERLOCK HOLMES

Diamond, S.Z. and McKay, M. (eds), *Serpentine Musings, Volume One* (Gasogene Books, 2004)

——, *Serpentine Musings, Volume Two* (Gasogene Books, 2005)

Rice, S., 'Dubious and Questionable Memories: A History of the Adventuresses of Sherlock Holmes', *The Baker Street Journal Christmas Annual 2004* (The Baker Street Irregulars, 2004)

THE BAKER STREET IRREGULARS (THE BSI HISTORY PROJECT)

Nieminski, J. and Lellenberg, J.L. (eds), *'Dear Starrett—' 'Dear Briggs—': A Compendium of Correspondence Between Vincent Starrett and Gray Chandler Briggs (1930–1934)* (The Baker Street Irregulars, 1989)

Lellenberg, J.L. (ed.), *Irregular Memories of the 'Thirties: An Archival History of the Baker Street Irregulars' First Decade, 1930–1940* (The Baker Street Irregulars, 1990)

—, *Irregular Records of the Early 'Forties: An Archival History of the Baker Street Irregulars, January 1941–March 1944* (The Baker Street Irregulars, 1991)

—, *Irregular Proceedings of the Mid 'Forties: An Archival History of the Baker Street Irregulars, Autumn 1943–June 1947* (The Baker Street Irregulars, 1995)

—, '"Entertainment and Fantasy": The 1940 BSI Dinner', *The Baker Street Journal Christmas Annual 1998* (The Baker Street Irregulars, 1998)

—, *Irregular Crises of the Late 'Forties: An Archival History of the Baker Street Irregulars, Summer 1947–December 1950* (The Baker Street Irregulars, 1999)

—, *Disjecta Membra: Stray Scraps of Irregular History, 1932–1950* (The Baker Street Irregulars, 2001)

—, *'Certain Rites and Also Certain Duties': Unsuspected Sources of Baker Street Irregularity* (Hazelbaker & Lellenberg Inc., 2009)

• SOME RECOMMENDED WEBSITES •

THE STORIES OF SHERLOCK HOLMES

www.ignisart.com/camdenhouse/ – The texts of all sixty stories, plus a huge collection of Holmesian graphics, and more.
http://sherlockholmes.stanford.edu/readings.html – Twelve stories from *The Strand Magazine* in facsimile, with notes and more information.

GENERAL

www.sherlockian.net – Christopher Redmond's site is the best and most comprehensive.

www.fastol.com/~renkwitz/disjecta_membra.htm – *Disjecta Membra* is another good place to start.

www.bestofsherlock.com/index.htm – Randall Stock's site is invaluable for information about Conan Doyle manuscripts, copies of *Beeton's Christmas Annual 1887*, and original artwork by Paget, Steele, et al.

www.schoolandholmes.com/sherlockiana.html – Adrian Nebbett's site contains indexes to twenty-six important books from *The Annotated Sherlock Holmes* by William S. Baring-Gould to *Sherlock Holmes and Music* by Guy Warrack.

http://special.lib.umn.edu/rare/ush/ush.html – *The Universal Sherlock Holmes* is Ronald De Waal's monumental bibliography.

www.tc.umn.edu/~bergq003/holmes/index.htm – *Sherlockian Resources on the Internet: A Survey*, by John Bergquist.

http://artintheblood.com/scan2/scantitle.htm – *Art in the Blood* is L.M. Goode's site, devoted to Sidney Paget and other illustrators of the Canon.

http://sherlocktron.hostoi.com/scuttle.htm – *Scuttlebutt from the Spermaceti Press* is an archive of Peter Blau's Sherlockian newsletter from 1985 to the present.

www.sherlock-holmes.org.uk/district.php – *The District Messenger* is an archive of the Sherlock Holmes Society of London's newsletter from 1982 to the present.

www.sherlocknews.com – *Sherlock Holmes News* is Charles Prepolec's Holmes and Conan Doyle blog.

THE HISTORICAL AND SOCIAL BACKGROUND

www.victorianlondon.org – *Victorian London* is Lee Jackson's amazingly comprehensive encyclopaedia.

SIR ARTHUR CONAN DOYLE

www.siracd.com/index.shtml – *The Chronicles of Sir Arthur Conan Doyle.*

www.the-conan-doyle-crowborough-establishment.com – The Conan Doyle (Crowborough) Establishment is especially helpful for Conan Doyle's years living at Crowborough.

http://saveundershaw.com – The Undershaw Preservation Trust includes details of Conan Doyle's years spent at Hindhead.

COLLECTIONS

http://elisanonline.com/sublibrarians/index.html – A list of Sherlock Holmes and Arthur Conan Doyle collections held in public and academic libraries, compiled by the Sub-Librarians' Scion of the Baker Street Irregulars.

www.torontopubliclibrary.ca/books-video-music/specialized-collections/literature-genre-doyle.jsp – The Arthur Conan Doyle Collection at Toronto Reference Library.

www.westminster.gov.uk/services/libraries/special/sher-
lock – The Sherlock Holmes Collection at Marylebone
Library, London.

http://special.lib.umn.edu/rare/holmes.phtml – The
Sherlock Holmes Collections at the University of
Minnesota, Minneapolis.

www.bsitrust.org – The Baker Street Irregulars Trust collection at Harvard University.

www.conandoylecollection.co.uk – The Conan Doyle
Collection (Lancelyn Green Bequest) at Portsmouth.

www.acdfriends.org – Friends of the Arthur Conan Doyle
Collection, Toronto Public Library.

SOCIETIES

www.ash-nyc.com – The Adventuresses of Sherlock
Holmes.

www.bsiarchivalhistory.org/BSI_Archival_History/
Welcome.html – Jon Lellenberg's 'Archival History of the
Baker Street Irregulars'.

www.bakerstreetjournal.com – *The Baker Street Journal*

www.beaconsociety.com – The Beacon Society: 'dedicated to supporting educational experiences which
introduce young people to the study of Sherlock
Holmes literature'.

www.torontobootmakers.com – The Bootmakers of Toronto.

www.byskovjensen.com/cimbrian – The Cimbrian Friends
of Baker Street.

www.thessmayday.org.uk – The Crew of the S.S. May Day.

www.sherlockholmes.cz – The Czech Society of Sherlock Holmes.

www.holmesjapan.jp/english – Japan Sherlock Holmes Club.

http://minitonga.thing.com – The Mini-Tonga Society: making Holmes's world in miniature.

www.poorfolk.co.uk – The Poor Folk upon the Moors.

www.221b.ch/index_e.html – The Reichenbach Irregulars.

http://sherlockscotland.com – The Self-Important Scotland Yarders: the Sherlock Holmes Society of Scotland.

www.sherlock-holmes.org.uk – The Sherlock Holmes Society of London.

www.sshf.com – La Société Sherlock Holmes de France.

http://soundofthebaskervilles.com – The Sound of the Baskervilles.

http://thestormypetrels.com – The Stormy Petrels of British Columbia.

www.sherlock.on.net – The Sydney Passengers.

www.sh-whoswho.com/index.php – Sherlockian Who's Who.

http://sherlockholmes.ning.com – The Sherlock Holmes Social Network.

www.bcpl.net/~lmoskowi/hounds/hounds.html – The Hounds of the Internet.

MUSEUMS AND EXHIBITIONS

www.westminsteronline.org/holmes1951 – Sherlock Holmes Exhibition held at Abbey House, Baker Street in 1951.

www.myswitzerland.com/en/sherlock-holmes-museum-meiringen.html – Sherlock Holmes Museum, Meiringen, Switzerland.

www.lucens.ch/TOUR/Sherlock.html – Sherlock Holmes Museum, Lucens, Switzerland.

www.sherlockiana.dk/shklub/museum_en.shtml – Sherlock Holmes Museum, Nykøbing Sj., Denmark.

www.sherlockholmespub.com – The Sherlock Holmes pub and restaurant, London.

www.sherlock-holmes.fr/murder-party/2-a-visit.htm – Sherlock Holmes Museum, Saint-Sauvier, France.

www.sherlock-holmes.co.uk – Sherlock Holmes Museum, London.

http://221bbakerstreetla.com/index.asp – Chuck Kovacik's full-sized recreation of the sitting-room at 221B.

PODCASTS

www.ihearofsherlock.com – 'I Hear of Sherlock Everywhere': interviews with major Sherlockians and others.

http://bakerstreetbabes.podomatic.com – The Baker Street Babes: interviews and discussions by the Babes.

DRAMA

www.imdb.com/character/ch0026631 – Internet Movie Database: Holmes on screen.

www.bertcoules.co.uk/intro.htm – The BBC Radio 4 complete Sherlock Holmes.

www.sherlockology.com – 'Sherlockology': unofficial but approved site devoted to BBC's *Sherlock*.

www.sherlock-holmes.org.uk/world/radio.php – Audio dramas presented by the Sherlock Holmes Society of London.